THE BOOK OF FORBIDDEN KNOWLEDGE

BLACK MAGIC, SUPERSTITIONS, CHARMS, DIVINATION, SIGNS, OMENS, ETC.

Johnson Smith & Company

2023 Edition of the original book published before 1923.

ISBN: 979-8378262755

Any person fasting on midsummer eve, and sitting' on the church porch, will, at midnight, see the spirits of the persons of that parish, who will die that year, come and knock at the church-door, in the order and succession in which they will die. One of those watchers, there being several in company, fell into a profound sleep, so that he could not be waked; whilst in this state his ghost was seen by the rest of his companions knocking at the church door. Any unmarried woman fasting on midsummer eve, and at midnight laying a clean cloth, with bread, cheese and ale, and sitting down as if going to eat, the street door being left open, the person whom she is afterward to marry -will come into the room, and drink to her by bowing, and afterward filling the glass, will leave it on the table, and making another bow, retire. On St. Agnes' night, the 21st of January, take a row of pins, and pull out every one, one after another, saying a paternoster, on sticking a pin in your sleeve, and you will dream of him you shall marry. Another method to see a future spouse in a dream; the party inquiring must lie in a different country from that in which he commonly resides, and, on going to bed, must knit the left garter about the right legged stocking, letting the other garter and stocking alone; and as you rehearse the following verses, at every comma knit a knot: This knot I knit, To know a thing I know not yet, That I may see The man that shall my husband be, How he goes and what he wears, And what he does all days and years. Accordingly, in a dream he will appear with the insignia of his trade or profession. Another performed by charming the moon, thus: At the first appearance of the new moon, immediately after the new year's day, go out in the evening and stand over the spears of a gate or stile, and, looking on the moon, repeat the following lines: All hail to thee, moon; all hail to thee, I prithee, good moon, reveal to me This night who my husband must be. The party will then dream of their future husband. A slice of the bridecake, thrice thrown through the wedding ring, and laid under the head of an unmarried woman will make them dream of their future husband. The same is practiced in the north with a piece of the groaning cheese.

HOW TO RECEIVE ORACLES BY DREAM

He who would receive true dreams, should keep a pure, undisturbed, and imaginative spirit, and so compose it that it may be made worthy of knowledge and government by the mind; for such a spirit is most fit for prophesying, and is a most clear glass of all things. When, therefore, we are sound in body, not disturbed in mind, our intellect not made dull by heavy meals and strong drink, not sad through poverty, not provoked through lust, not incited by any vice, not stirred up by wrath or anger, not being irreligiously and profanely inclined, not given to levity nor lost in drunkenness, but, chastely going to bed, fall asleep, then our pure and divine soul being free from all the evils above recited, and separated from all hurtful thoughts — and now freed, by dreaming — is endowed with this divine spirit as an instrument, and doth receive those beams and representations which are darted down, as it were, and shine forth from the divine Mind into itself, in a deifying glass There are four kinds of true dreams, Viz., the first, matutine, i.e., between sleeping' and waking; the second, that which one sees concerning' another; the third, that whose interpretation is shown to the same dreamer in the nocturnal vision; and, lastly, that which is related to the same dreamer in the nocturnal vision. But natural thing's and their own co-mixtures do likewise belong unto wise men, and we often use such to receive oracles from a spirit by a dream, which are neither by perfumes, unctions, meats, drinks, rings, seals, etc. Now those who are desirous to receive oracles through a dream, let them make themselves a ring of the Sun or Saturn for this purpose. There are likewise images of dreams, which, being put under the head when going to sleep, doth effectually give true dreams of whatever the mind hath before determined or consulted upon, the practice of which is as follows: Thou shalt make an image of the Sun, the figure whereof must be a man sleeping upon the bosom of an angel; which thou shalt make -when Leo ascends, the Sun being in the ninth house In Aries; then you must write upon the figure the name of the effect desired, and in the hand of the angel the name and character of the intelligence of the Sun, which is Michael. Let the same image be made in Virgo ascending — Mercury being fortunate in Aries in the ninth, or Gemini ascending, Mercury being fortunate in the ninth house in Aquarius — and let him be received by Saturn with a fortunate aspect, and let the name of the spirit (Which is Raphael) be written upon it. Let the same likewise be made — -Libra ascending, "Venus being received from Mercury in Gemini in the ninth house — and write upon it the name of the angel of Venus (which is Anael). Again you may make the same image — Aquarius ascending, Saturn fortunately possessing the ninth in his exaltation, which is Libra — and let there be written upon it the name of the angel of Saturn (which is Cassial). The same may be made with Cancer ascending, the Moon being received by Jupiter and Venus in Pisces, and being fortunately placed in the ninth house — and write upon it the spirit of the Moon (which Is Gabriel). There are likewise made rings of dreams of wonderful efficacy, and there are rings of the Sun and Saturn — and the constellation of them is, when the Sun or Saturn ascend in their exaltation in the ninth, and when the Moon Is joined to Saturn in the ninth, and in that sign which was the ninth house of the nativity, and write and engrave upon the rings the name of the spirit of the Sun or Saturn, and by these rules you may know how and by what means to constitute more of yourself. But know this, that such images work nothing (as they are simply images), except they are vivified by spiritual and celestial virtue, and chiefly by the ardent desire and firm intent of the soul of the operator. But who can give a soul to an image, or make a stone, or metal, or clay, or wood, or wax, or paper, to live? Certainly no man whatever, for this arcanum doth not enter into an artist of a stiff neck. He only hath it who transcends the progress of angels, and comes to the very Archtype Himself. The tables of numbers likewise confer to the receiving of oracles, being duly formed under their own constellations. Therefore, he who is desirous of receiving true oracles by dreams, let him abstain from supper, from drink, and be otherwise well disposed, so his brain will be free from turbulent vapors; let him also have his bed-chamber fair and clean, exorcised and consecrated; then let him perfume the same with some convenient fumigation, and let him anoint his temples with some unguent efficacious hereunto, and put a ring of dreams upon his finger; then let him take one of the images we have spoken of, and place the same under his head; then let him address himself to sleep, meditating upon that thing which he desires to know. So shall he receive a most certain and undoubted oracle by a dream when the Moon goes through the sign of the ninth revolution of his nativity, and she is in the ninth .sign from the sign of perfection. This is the way whereby we may obtain all sciences and arts whatsoever, whether astrology, occult philosophy, physic, etc., or else suddenly and perfectly with a true illumination of our intellect, although all inferior familiar spirits whatsoever conduce to this effect, and sometimes also evil spirits sensibly inform us, intrinsically and extrinsically.

DREAMS, TOKENS, AND INSIGHTS INTO FUTURITY

THE RING AND THE OLIVE BRANCH

Buy a ring; it matters not it being gold, so as it has the semblance of a wedding ring; and it is best to try this charm on your own birthday. Pay for your ring with some small bill, for whatever change you receive you must give it to the first beggar you meet in the street; and, if no one asks alms of you, give it to some poor person — for you need not, alas! go far before you find one to whom your charity will be acceptable; carefully note what they say in return, such as "God bless you," or wishing you luck and prosperity, as is usual. When you get home, write it down on a sheet of paper, at each of four corners, and, in the middle, put the two first letters of your name, your age, and the letters of the planets then reigning as morning and evening stars, get a branch of olive and fasten the ring on the stalk with a string of thread which has been steeped all day in a mixture of honey and vinegar, or any composition of opposite qualities, very sweet and very sour; cover your ring and stalk with the written paper, carefully wrapped round and round; wear it in your bosom till the ninth hour of the night; then repair to the next church-yard and bury the charm in the grave of a young man who died unmarried; and, while you are so doing repeat the letters of your own Christian name three times backwards, return home, and keep as silent as possible till you go to bed, which must be done before eleven; put a light in your chimney, or some safe place, and, before midnight, or just about that time, your husband that is to be will present himself at the foot of the bed, but will presently disappear. If you are not to marry, none will come, and, in that case, if you dream before morning of children, it shows that you will have them unmarried; and if you dream of crowds of men, beware of prostitution.

THE WITCH'S CHAIN

Let three young women join together in making a long chain — about a yard will do — of Christmas juniper and mistletoe berries, and, at the end of every link, put an oak acorn. Exactly before midnight let them assemble in a room by themselves, where no one can disturb them; leave a window open, and take the key out of the keyhole and hang it over the chimney-piece; have a good fire, and place in the midst of it a long, thinnish log of wood, well sprinkled with oil, salt, and fresh mould; then wrap the chain round it, each maiden having an equal share in the business; then sit down, and on your left knee let each fair one have a prayer-book opened at the matrimonial service. Just as the last acorn is burned, the future husband will cross the room; each one will see her own proper spouse, but he will be invisible to the rest of the wakeful virgins. Those that are not be wed will see a coffin, or some misshapen form, cross the room; go to bed instantly, and you will all have remarkable dreams. This must he done either on a "Wednesday or Friday night, but no other.

LOVE'S CORDIAL

(To be tried the third night of a new moon.) Take brandy, rum, gin, wine, and the oil of amber, of each a teaspoonful; a tablespoonful of cream, and three of spring water; drink it as you get into bed. Repeat: This mixture of love I take for my potion, That I of my destiny may have a notion; Cupid befriend me, new moon be kind, And show unto me that fate that's designed. You will dream of drink, and, according to the quality or manner of it being presented, you may tell the condition to which you will rise or fall by marriage. Water is poverty; and if you dream of a drunken man, it is ominous that you will have a drunken mate. If you dream of drinking too much you will fall, at a future period, into that sad error yourself, without great care; and what is a worse sight than an inebriated female? She cannot guard her own honor, ruins her own and family's substance, and often clothes herself with rags. Trouble is often used as an excuse for this vicious habit; but it gives more trouble than it takes away.

LOVE LETTERS

On receiving a love letter that has any particular declaration in it, lay it wide open; then fold it in nine folds, pin it next your heart, and thus wear it till bedtime; then place it in your left-hand glove, and lay it under your head. If you dream of gold, diamonds, or any costly gems, your lover is true, and means what he says; if of white linen, you will lose him by death; and if of flowers, he will prove false. If you dream of his saluting you, he is, at present, false, and means not what he professes, but only to draw you into a snare.

MAGIC ROSE

Gather your rose on the 27th of June; let it be full blown, and as bright a red as you can get; pluck it between the hours of three and four in the morning, taking care to have no witness of the transaction; convey it to your chamber, and hold it over a chaffing dish or any convenient utensil for the purpose, in which there is charcoal and sulphur or brimstone; hold your rose over the smoke about Ave minutes, and you will see it have & wonderful effect on the flower. Before the rose gets the least cool, clap it in a sheet of writing paper, on -which is written your own name and that of the young man you love best; also the date of the year and the name of the morning star that has the ascendency at that time; fold it up and seal it neatly with three separate seals, then run and bury the parcel at the foot of the tree from which you gathered the flower; here let it remain untouched till the 6th of July; take it up at midnight, go to bed and place it under your pillow, and you will have a singular and most eventful dream before morning, or, at least, before your usual time of rising. You may keep the rose under your head three nights without spoiling the charm; when you are done with the rose and paper be sure to burn them.

LUCKY AND UNLUCKY DAYS, ETC.

LIST OF UNLUCKY DAYS

Which, to those persons being males born on them, will generally prove unfortunate: January 3, 4.
February 6, 7, 12, 13, 19, 20.
March 5, 6, 12, 13.
May 12, 13, 20, 21, 26, 27.
June 1, 2, 9, 10, 16, 17, 22, 23, 24.
July 3, 4, 10, 11, 16, 17, 18.
October 3, 4, 9, 10, 11, 16, 17, 31.
November 1, 3.

Almost all persons (being of the male sex) that are born on the days included in the foregoing table, will, In a greater or less degree suffer, not only by pecuniary embarrassment and losses of property, but will also experience great distress and anxiety of mind, much dissatisfaction, dissension, and unhappiness in their family affairs, much disaffection to each other among the married ones, (indeed few of them can ever be happy in the married state), trouble about their children, daughters forming unfortunate attachments, and a variety of untoward events of other description which our limits do not allow us to particularize. The influence of these days are of a quality and tendency calculated to excite in the minds of persons born on them, an extraordinary itch for speculation, to make changes in their affairs, commence new undertakings of various kinds, but all of them will tend nearly to one point — loss of property and pecuniary embarrassments. Such persons who embark their capital on credit in new concerns or engagements will be likely to receive checks or interruptions to the progress of their schemes or undertakings. Those who enter into engagements intended to be permanent, whether purchases, lease's, partnerships, or, in short, any other speculation of a description which cannot readily be transferred, or got rid of will dearly repent their bargains. They will find their affairs from time to time much interrupted and agitated, and experience many disappointments in money matters, trouble through bills, and have need of all their activity and address to prop their declining credit. Indeed, almost all engagements and affairs that are entered upon by persons born on any of these days will receive some sort of check or obstruction. The greater number of those persons born on these days will be subject to weakness or sprains in the knees and ankles, also diseases and hurts in the legs.

LIST OF UNLUCKY DAYS

Which to those persons (being females) born on them will generally prove unfortunate: January 5, 6, 13, 14, 20, and 21.
February 2, 3, 9, 10, 16, 17, 22, and 23.
March 1, 2, 8, 9, 16, 17, 28, and 29.
April 24 and 26. May 1, 2, 9, 17, 22, 29, and 30.
June 5, 6, 12, 13, 18, and 19.
July 3 and 4.
September 9 and 16.
October 20 and 27.
November 9, 10, 21, 29, and 30.
December 6, 14, and 21.

We particularly advise all females born on these days to be extremely cautious of placing their affections too hastily, as they will be subject to dispointments and vexations in that respect. It will be better for them (in those matters) to be guided by the advice of their friends, rather than by their own feeling, they will be less fortunate in placing their affections, than in any other action of their lives, as many of these marriages will terminate in separations, divorces, etc. Their courtships will end in unhappy elopements, and other ways not necessary of explanation. Our readers must be well aware that affairs of importance begun at inauspicious times, by those who have been born at those periods when the stars shed their malign influence, can seldom, if ever, lead to much good; it is, therefore, that we endeavor to lay before them a correct statement drawn from accurate astrological information, in order that by strict attention and care, they may avoid falling into those perplexing labyrinths from which nothing but that care and attention can save them. The list of days we have above given, will be productive of hasty and clandestine marriages — marriages under untoward circumstances, perplexing attachments, and a natural consequence, the displeasure of friends, together with family broils, discussions and divisions. We now present our readers with a

LIST OF DAYS USUALLY CONSIDERED FORTUNATE

With respect to Courtship, Marriage, and Love Affairs in General — Persons that were born on the following

days may expect courtships and prospects of marriage, and which will have a happy termination. January 1, 2, 15, 26, 27, 28.
February 11, 21, 25, 26.
March 10, 24.
April 6, 15, 16, 20, 28. May 3, 13, 18, 31.
June 10, 11, 15, 22, 25. July 9, 14, 15, 18.
August 6, 7, 10, 11, 19, 20, 25.
September 4, 8, 9, 17, 18, 23.
October 3, 7, 16, 21, 22.
November 5, 14, 20.
December 14, 15, 19, 20, 22, 23, 25.

Although the greater number, or indeed, nearly all persons that are born on the days stated in the preceding list, will be likely to meet with a prospect of marriage, or become engaged in some love affair of more than ordinary importance, yet it must not be expected that the result will be the same with all of them; with some they will terminate in marriage — with others in disappointment — and some of them will be in danger of forming attachments that may prove of a somewhat troublesome description. We shall, therefore, in order to enable our readers to distinguish them, give a comprehensive and useful list, showing - which of them will be most likely to marry. Those born within the limits of the succeeding List of Hours, on any of the preceding days, will be the most likely to marry — or will, at least, have courtships that will be likely to have a happy termination.

LIST OF FORTUNATE HOURS

January 2d. From 30 minutes past 10 till 15 minutes past 11 in the morning; and from 15 minutes before 9 till 15 minutes before 11 at night.
15th. From 30 minutes past 9 till 15 minutes past 10 in the morning; and from 30 minutes past 7 till 15 minutes past 11 at night.
26th. From 30 minutes past 8 till 15 minutes past 9 in the morning; and from T till 15 minutes past 10 at night.

February 11th and 12th. From 30 minutes past 7 till 15 minutes past 8 in the morning; and from 15 minutes past 6 till 15 minutes before 9 at night.
21st. From 7 till 15 minutes before 8 in the morning;' and from 15 minutes past 5 till 15 minutes before 8 at night.
25th and 26th. From 15 minutes before 7 till 30 minutes past 7 in the morning; and from 15 minutes before 5 till 30 minutes past 7 in the evening.

March 10th. From 5 till 15 minutes before 6 in the morning; and from 4 in the afternoon till 15 minutes before 7 in the evening.

April 6th. From 15 minutes past 4 till 5 in the morning; and from 30 minutes past 2 till 15 minutes past a in the afternoon. 20th. From 30 minutes past 3 till 15 minutes past 4 in the morning; and from 30 minutes past 1 till 15 minutes past 4 in the afternoon.

May 3d. From 15 minutes before 3 till 30 minutes past 3 in the morning; and from 15 minutes before 1 till 30

minutes past 3 in the afternoon.
18th. From 2 till 15 minutes before 3 in the morning; and from 12 at noon till 15 minutes before 3 in the afternoon.
28th. From 15 minutes before 1 till 30 minutes past 2 in the morning; and from 15 minutes before 12 at noon till 30 minutes past 2 in the afternoon.
31st. From 15 minutes before 1 till 30 minutes past 1 in the morning; and. from 15 minutes past 10 in the morning till 15 minutes before 1 in the afternoon.

June 10th and 11th. From 15 minutes from 12 at night till 1 in the morning.
15th. From 10 in the morning till 2 in the afternoon; and from 15 minutes before 12 at night till 15 minutes before 1 in the morning.
25th. From 15 minutes past 9 in the morning till 12 at noon; and from 11 to 12 at night.
29th. From 9 in the morning till 15 minutes before 12 at noon; and from 15 minutes before 11 till 15 minutes before 12 at night.

July 9th. From 15 minutes past 8 till 11 in the morning; and from 10 till 11 at night. 14th and 15th. From 8 till 11 in the morning; and from 10 till 11 at night. 28th. From 7 till 10 in the morning; and from 9 till 10 at night.

August 6th and 7th. From 30 minutes past 6 till 15 minutes past 9 in the morning; and from 15 minutes past 8 till 15 minutes past 9 at night.
10th and 11th. From 15 minutes past 6 till 9 in the morning; and from 8 till 9 in the evening.
19th and 20th. From 30 minutes past 5 till 30 minutes

past 8 in the morning; and from 30 minutes past 7 till 30 minutes past 8 in the evening.
25th. From 15 minutes past 5 till 8 in the morning; and from 7 till 8 in the evening.

September 4th. From 15 minutes before 5 till 30 minutes past 7 in the morning; and from 30 minutes past 6 till 30 minutes past 7 in the evening.
8th and 9th. From 30 minutes past 4 till 15 minutes past 7 in the morning; and from 15 minutes past 6 till 15 minutes past 7 in the evening.
17th and 18th. From 5 till 15 minutes before 5 in the morning; and from 15 minutes before 6 till 15 minutes before 7 in the evening.
23d. From 30 minutes past 3 till 30 minutes past 5 in the morning; and from 30 minutes past 5 till 30 minutes past 6 in the evening.

October 3d. From 3 till 15 minutes before 6 in the morning; and from 15 minutes past 4 till 15 minutes past 5 in the afternoon. 7th. From 15 minutes before 3 till 30 minutes past 5 in the morning; and from 30 minutes past 4 till 30 minutes past 5 in the afternoon. 16th. From 2 till 5 in the morning; and from 4 till 5 in the afternoon
21st and 22d. From 15 minutes before 2 till 30 minutes past 4 in the morning 1 ; and from 30 minutes past 3 till 15 minutes past 4 in the afternoon.

November 5th. From 1 till 15 minutes before 4 in the morning; and from 15 minutes before 3 till 15 minutes before 4 in the afternoon.
14th. From 15 minutes past 12 till 3 in the morning'; and from 2 till 3 in the afternoon.

20th. From 15 minutes before 12 till 15 minutes past 2 in the morning-; and from 15 minutes past 1 till 2 in the afternoon.

December 14th and 15th. From 10 till 30 minutes past 12 in the morning; and from 12 at noon till 15 minutes before 1 in the afternoon.
18th and 19th. From 15 minutes before 10 at night till 15 minutes past 5 in the morning; and from 30 minutes past 11 till 15 minutes past 12 at night.

January 3d. From 30 minutes past 10 till 15 minutes past 11 in the morning; and from 15 minutes before 9 till 15 minutes past 11 at night.
12th and 13th. From 15 minutes past 9 till 10 in the morning; and from 15 minutes before 8 to 30 minutes past 10 at night.
18th. From 9 till 15 minutes before 10 in the morning; and from 15 minutes past 7 till 10 at night.
27th. From 9 till 15 minutes before 10 in the morning; and from 7 till 15 minutes before 10 at night.

February 1st. From 8 till 30 minutes past 8 in the morning; and from 6 till 30 minutes past 8 in the evening.
11th and 12th. From 15 minutes before 8 till 30 minutes past 8 in the morning; and from 15 minutes before 6 till 30 minutes past 8 in the evening.
17th. From 7 till 15 minutes before 8 in the morning; and from 15 minutes past 5 till 8 in the evening.

March 1st. From 30 minutes past 6 till 15 minutes past 7 in the morning; and from 30 minutes past 4 till 15 minutes past 7 in the evening.

16th and 17th. From 30 minutes past 5 till 15 minutes past 6 in the morning; and from 15 minutes before 4 till 30 minutes past 6 in the evening.

19th, 20th, 21st, 22d, 23d, 24th, and 25th. From 30 minutes past 5 till 30 minutes past 6 in the morning; and from 30 minutes past 3 till 15 minutes past 6 in the evening.

26th, 27th, 28th, 29th, and 30th. From 15 minutes past 5 till 15 minutes before 6 in the morning; and from 15 minutes past 3 till 6 in the evening.

April 3d, 4th, 5th, 6th, 7th, 8th, and 9th. From 30 minutes past 4 till 30 minutes past 5 in the morning; and from 30 minutes past 2 till 5 in the afternoon.

10th, 11th, 12th, 13th, and 14th. From 15" minutes before 4 till 15 minutes before 5 in the morning; and from 2 till 30 minutes past 4 in the afternoon.

19th, 20th, 21st, 22d, and 23d. From 30 minutes past 4 in the morning; and from 15 minutes before 2 till 30 minutes past 4 in the afternoon.

25th, 26th, 27th, and 28th. From 3 till 4 in the morning; and from 15 minutes past 1 till 15 minutes before 4 in the afternoon.

May 3d, 4th, 5th, 6th, 7th, and 8th. From 15 minutes past two till 15 minutes past 3 in the morning; and from 30 minutes past 12 at noon till 15 minutes past 3 in the afternoon.

9th, 10th, 11th, 12th. From 2 till 3 in the morning; and from 15 minutes past 12 at noon till 3 in the afternoon.

16th, 17th, 18th, 19th, 20th, 21st, and 22d. From 15 minutes before 2 till 15 minutes before 3 in the morning; and from 12 at noon till 15 minutes before 3 in the afternoon.

23d, 24th, 25th, 26th, and 27th. From 15 minutes past 1 till 15 minutes past 2 in the morning; and from 30 minutes past 11 in the forenoon till 15 minutes past 2 in the afternoon.

June 1st, 2d. 3d, 4th, 5th, and 6th. From 15 minutes past 10 in the morning till 1 in the afternoon; and from 15 minutes past 12 at night till 15 minutes past 1 the next morning.
11th. From 15 minutes past 10 in the morning till 15 minutes before 1 in the afternoon; and from 12 at night till 1 the next morning.
20th. From 30 minutes past 9 in the morning till 12 at noon; and from 11 till 12 at night.
25th. From 15 minutes past nine in the morning till 15 minutes past 12 at noon; and from 11 till 12 at night.

July 5th. From 15 minutes before 8 till 15 minutes past 10 in the morning; and from 15 minutes before 10 till 15 minutes before 11 at night.
9th. From 15 minutes past 8 till 11 in the morning; and from 15 minutes past 10 till 11 at night.
19th. From 30 minutes past 7 till 10 in the morning; and from 15 minutes past 9 till 15 minutes past 10 at night.
24th. From 7 till 15 minutes before 10 in the morning; and from 9 till 10 at night.

August 2d and 3d. From 30 minutes past 6 till 15 minutes before 9 in the morning; and from 30 minutes past 8 till 30 minutes past 9 at night.
6th. From 15 minutes before 6 till 9 in the morning; and from 30 minutes past 7 till 30 minutes past 8 at night.

22d. From 15 minutes past 5 till 8 in the morning; and from 15 minutes past 7 till 15 minutes past 8 at night.

September 1st. From 4 till 15 minutes before 7 in the morning; and 6 till 7 in the evening.
5th. From 30 minutes past 4 till 15 minutes before 7 in the morning; and from 30 minutes past 6 till 30 minutes past 7 in the evening.
14th. From 15 minutes before 4 till 30 minutes past 6 in the morning; and from 30 minutes past 5 till 30 minutes past 6 in the evening.
29th. From 15 minutes before 3 till 30 minutes past 5 in the morning; and from 30 minutes past 4 till 30 minutes past 5 in the evening.

October 3d. From 3 till 15 minutes before 6 in the morning; and from 15 minutes before 5 till 15 minutes before 6 in the evening.
12th. From 15 minutes past 3 till 5 in the morning; and from 15 minutes before 4 till 30 minutes past 4 in the afternoon.
18th and 19th. From 30 minutes past 1 till 4 in the morning; and from 15 minutes before 3 till 30 minutes past 4 in the afternoon.

November 10th and 11th. From 30 minutes past 12 at night till 15 minutes past 3 in the morning; and from 30 minutes past 1 till 30 minutes past 2 in the afternoon.
15th and 16th. From 12 at night till 15 minutes before 3 in the morning; and from 15 minutes past 1 till 2 in the afternoon.
29th and 30th. From 15 minutes past 11 at night till 2 in the morning; and from 1 till 15 minutes before 2 in

the afternoon.

December 8th and 9th. From 15 minutes past 10 at night till 1 in the morning; and from 30 minutes past 12 at noon till 30 minutes past 1 in the afternoon.
14th, 15th, and 16th. From 10 at night till 15 minutes before 1 in the morning; and from 15 minutes before 12 till 30 minutes past 12 at noon.
23d and 24th. From 15 minutes past 11 till 12 at noon; and from 15 minutes past 9 till 12 at night.
28th. From 15 minutes past 10 till 11 in the morning; and from 9 till 15 minutes before 12 at night.

We do not presume to assert that every person born on the last mentioned times, will be exempt from all descriptions of trouble during the whole of their lives, but that they will never (in spite of whatever may happen to befall them) sink below mediocrity. Even servants and those born of poor parents will possess some superior qualities — get into good company — be much noticed by their superiors, and Will, in spite of any intervening difficulties, establish themselves in the world, and rise much above their sphere of birth. It has often been recorded, and though a singular observation, experience has shown it to be a true one, that some event of importance is sure to happen to a woman in her thirty-first year, whether single or married; it may prove for her good, or it may be some great evil or temptation; therefore we advise her to be cautious and circumspect in all her actions. If she is a maiden or widow, it is probable she will marry this year. If a wife that she will lose her children or her husband. She will either receive riches or travel into a foreign land; at all events, some circumstance or other will take place during this remarkable year of her life, that will have great effect on her future fortunes and existence. The like is applicable to men in their forty-second year, of which so many instances have been proved that there is not a doubt of its truth: Observe always to take a leasc for an odd number of years; even are not prosperous. — The three first days of the moon are the best for signing papers, and the first five days as well as the twenty-fourth for any fresh undertaking. But we cannot but allow that a great deal depends on our own industry and perseverance, and by strictly discharging our duty to God and man. we may often overcome the malign influence of a bad planet, or a day marked as unlucky in the book of fate.

METRAGRAMMATISM

OR THE ART OF FORTUNE-TELLING BY TRANSPOSITION OF NAMES

It has often been remarked, although it is a fact by no means commonly known, that the names given to children at the baptismal font joined to their family or surnames, and added to titles which may be bestowed upon them in after life, often point out many circumstances and events which may befall the parties upon whom such names have been bestowed; and that if their parents had paid more attention to this part of Astrological divination, those names which were unlucky might, by due care and attention, have been avoided, while those of a more fortunate description might have been selected for their children, and have been rendered even still more valuable and fortunate, by being conjoined with others of a like nature. In order that our readers may have a clearer insight into this branch of fortune-telling, and which appears to have been strangely neglected by modern practitioners, we shall lay "before them a few specimens of this admirable system of discovering the events of our checkered existence; and from a study of which they will readily learn how to avoid bestowing on their children such as are of a malignant nature; and, at the same time, perceive how 8 the secret influence of the stars that preside at our birth, act in the minutest manner — even to the giving of that name at our baptism, which oftentimes explains to the bearer of it, if he could then but know it, those events which will assuredly befall him in the course of his life. Of the antiquity of this science it is scarcely necessary to speak

— it may however be as -well to remark, that it was formerly in the highest repute among the astrologers of the early ages, and even some of our ancient writers have not disdained to advocate its cause. One of these, the celebrated Camden, has in his "Remains" bequeathed to the "world an excellent treatise on this subject. He refers the origin of this invention tc the time of Moses, and conceives that it might have had some share in the mystical tradition afterward called Cabalo, communicated by that divine lawgiver to the chosen seventy. — That this art was practiced by the ancient Egyptians there cannot be a doubt, as there are even now remaining several of the names of the Egyptian monarchs which have been transposed and fully point out the principal events of their lives. The Greeks also practiced the art, but we do not find any examples among the Romans, which is somewhat surprising, as their seers, astrologers, and sybils practiced almost every species of divination. Among modern nations, the French appear to have distinguished themselves for their proficiency in it, and which, Camden says, "they exceedingly admire and celebrate for the deep antiquity and mystical meaning thereof." Indeed, to such a height did that nation carry the practice of this art in the early ages, that there were kept lists of lucky and unlucky names, and particular care was taken, when bestowing a name on a child, that such only should be given as could, by transposition, be formed into some fortunate signification. But this often failed, for even those very names which, when transposed, contained this fortunate signification; yet, by a second transposition, sometimes quite the contrary would be indicated and thus "Foil those, who would have foil'd the stars." Having thus introduced this subject to our readers, and fully proved its antiquity, it only remains for us to lay before them such specimens of the art as may enable them to practice upon their own names, and by so doing become acquainted with that principal occurrence of their lives, which may be for their future good or evil; and if the latter, by possessing such foreknowledge, by caution and good conduct on their parts, alleviate or prevent its affects. We shall take these instances from the names of well known characters, by which it will be instantly seen how immediate is the connection between the name of the party and the principal event of their lives. And first with the name of Bonaparte, which is perhaps the most complete specimen of the art we could possibly lay before our readers, and if properly transposed fully shows in each transposition the character of the man, and points out that unfortunate occurrence in his life, which ultimately proved his ruin — thus: NAPOLEON BONAPARTE. NO, APPEAR NOT ON ELBA. In the name of Wellington we find his future glory parts: ARTHUR WELLESLEY, Duke of Wellington. LET WELL FOILED GAUL secure thy renown. And the like in that of Nelson, — thus: HORATIO NELSON. HONOR EST A NILO. Which in English means "Honor is to be found at the Nile!" In the name of SIR FRANCIS BURDETT we find: FRANTIC DISTURBERS, which fully prophesies the busy scenes' of popular riot and disturbance in which he would be engaged. In the name of the late lamented Princess Charlotte, we have another proof of the infallibility of this art — thus: PRINCESS CHARLOTTE AUGUSTA OF WALES, P. HER AUGUST RACE IS LOST, O! FATAL NEWS! The following anagram on James VI of Scotland, fully proves that his future fortune was predicted at his baptism — thus : CHARLES JAMES STUART CLAIMS ARTHUR'S SEAT, and accordingly, on the death of Queen Elizabeth, he became James I. of England, and thereby possessed the throne which the name given him at his birth plainly foretold! The above will be sufficient to instruct our readers in this very entertaining and infallible mode of discovering future events. It may be necessary to observe, that some names will not easily form into separate words without the addition or subtraction of one or more letters, this is always allowable — for instance, K may be substituted for C — I for J — V for U— and vice versa. These specimens will be sufficient to prove the infallibility of this art; and many of our readers will find, if they transpose the letters of their own names after the same fashion, that their future good or ill fortune will be thereby plainly pointed out.

DAYS OF THE WEEK

1. Their importance at the natal hour. A child born on Sunday will be of long life and obtain riches. A child born on Monday will be weak and effeminate. Tuesday is more unfortunate still though a child born on this day may, by extraordinary vigilance, conquer the inordinate desires to which he will be subject; still, in his reckless attempts to gratify them, he will be in danger of a violent death. The child born on Wednesday will be given to a studious life, and shall reap great profit therefrom. A child born on Thursday shall attain great honor and dignity. He who calls Friday his natal day shall be of a strong constitution, and perhaps addicted to the pleasures of love. Saturday is another ill-omened day; most children born on this day will be of heavy, dull, and dogged dispositions. II. Their influence otherwise. If a person have his measure taken for new clothes on a Sunday, he will be sorrowful and crying. If on a Monday, he will have ample food and provisions. If on a Tuesday, his clothes will be burned. If on a Wednesday, he will enjoy happiness and tranquility. If on Thursday, he will be good and propitious. If on a Friday, he will get into prison. If on Saturday, he will experience numerous troubles and misfortunes. If one puts on a new suit of clothes on a Sunday, he will experience happiness and ease. If on a Monday, his clothes will tear. If on a Tuesday, even if he stand in water, his clothes will catch fire. If on a Wednesday, he will readily obtain a new suit. If on a Thursday, his dress will appear neat and elegant. If on a Friday, as long as the suit remains new, he will be happy and delighted. If on a Saturday, he will be taken ill. If a person puts

on a new suit of clothes in the morning, he will become wealthy and fortunate. If at noon, he will appear elegant. If at about sunset, he will become wretched. If in the evening, he will continue ill. If a person bathe on Sunday, he will experience affliction. If on Monday, his property will increase. If on Tuesday, he will labor under anxiety of mind. If on Wednesday,, he will increase in beauty. If on Thursday, his property will increase. If on Friday, all his sins will be forgiven him. If on Saturday, all his ailments will be removed. For shaving, four days of the week are preferable to the rest, viz., Monday, Wednesday, Thursday, and Friday; the other three are evil and inauspicious. Lucky days for business, three first days of the moon's age; for marriage the 7th, 9th, and 12th; requesting favors, 14th, lath, and 17th, but beware the 16th and 21st; to answer letters, if possible choose an odd day of the moon; to travel on land, choose the increase of the moon; and to embark on the ocean, choose the decline. March is a fortunate month for beginning a new building; and it is singular, but nevertheless reckoned true, that it is good to open a concert-room, a music-shop, or begin a new piece of music on the eve of St. Cecilia. It is not good to marry on your own birthday, or on any martyr's; every other saint's day is fortunate in this concern; neither is it fortunate for a woman to marry in colors; let her dress be as white as possible, except she be a widow, then let her choose some pleasant color, but beware of green and yellow. To meet a funeral as you are going to church to tie the nuptial knot, betokens the death of your first child in its infancy. To meet a white horse when you are going on any particular business is a sign of success, and a piebald one, if you are going to ask a favor; to be followed by a strange dog is lucky, especially to a man who is going courting. For a pigeon to fly into the house not belonging to it is a sign of sickness, and if it rests on a bed, it is death, but two pigeons is a sign of a wedding. Never pick up an odd glove in the street; it is not fortunate. Never tell any dream before breakfast, nor any at all that you use a charm to procure, even to your most trusty friend. If you dream any dream three times, look on it as an omen of friendly warning, particularly if it regard water, traveling, or any other perilous business. It may be intended by a watchful Providence to save you from danger, so do not despise the caution. There are several remarkable instances in history— such as William the Second, the Duke of Buckingham, and many others — who might have escaped death at that time by a due attention to these warnings.

SECRETS OF BLACK MAGIC REVEALED

WHEN A PERSON DESIRES TO REMOVE CORNS

When they bury an old man, and the funeral bells are ringing, the following should be spoken: They are sounding the funeral bell and what I now grasp may soon be well and what ill I grasp do take away, like the dead one in the grave does lay. While reciting the sentence, always hold the troubled part in the hand, and regarding the corns, move over them with your fingers after cutting out the corns, and as long as they are tolling the bells repeat the above. As soon as the dead body begins to bleach the corns will disappear. Probate in the case of a male, wait for the funeral of one of that sex; in the case of a female wait until a female is to be buried.

WHEN A SORE FAILS TO BREAK OPEN

Take virgin-parchments as large as the sore, put it first in water and then on the sore spot. Propatum!

FOR FRESH WOUNDS

Fresh is the wound, blessed is the day! happy the hour I found soon to stop and arrest thee, so that thou neither swell nor fester until mountains meet.

TO STAY A SHOT

Shot stand still in the name of the Lord, give neither Are nor flame, as sure as the rock of Gibraltar remains firm. While dissolving it, say: "God saw his joy and glory!"

TO COMPEL, A THIEF TO RETURN THE STOLEN PROPERTY

Obtain a new earthen pot with a cover, draw water from the under current of a stream while calling out the three holiest names. Fill the vessel one-third, take the same to your home, set it upon the fire, take a piece of bread from the lower crust of a loaf, stick three pins into the bread, boil all in the vessel, add a few dew nettles. Then say: Thief, male or female, bring my stolen articles back, whether thou art boy or girl; thief, if thou art woman or man, I compel thee, in the name.

TO MAKE A MAGNETIC COMPASS WHICH WILL SERVE TO DISCOVER THE TREASURES AND ORES IN THE EARTH

For this purpose a magnet made of the plusquam perfection, accompanied by the prime material of which all metals grow is requisite; with this, the magnet of the compass must be strengthened. Around the compass are engraved the characteristic signs of all the seven metals. If it is desired now to ascertain what kind of a metal is most likely to be found in a hidden treasure or in ore beneath the earth, it will be only necessary to hie to that particular spot, where the magnetic rod has given the indication, but you must put your foot there where the perpendicular shows its attraction, and take of every metal a small piece, that is, one as heavy as the other, and lay it upon the respective character and the needle will rotate to that metal which predominates under the surface of the earth, and there it will stand still.

TO DISCERN IN A MIRROR, WHAT AN ENEMY DESIGNS AT THE DISTANCE OF THREE MILES OR MORE

Obtain a good plain looking glass, as large as you please, and have it framed on three sides only; upon the left side it should be left open. Such a glass must be held toward the direction where the enemy is existing and you will be able to discern all his markings, maneuverings, his doings and workings. Was effectually used during the Thirty Years' war.

FOR VIOLENT TOOTHACHES

Take a new nail, pick with this the tooth till it bleeds, then take this nail and insert it in a place where neither sun or moon ever shines into, perhaps, in the rafters of the bin in a cellar, toward the rising of the sun; at the first stroke upon the nail call the name of him whom you design to help, and speak: Toothache fly away, by the second stroke: Toothache cease, pain allay!

EYEWATER WHICH MAKES THE SIGHT CLEAR, SO THAT NO SPECTACLES ARE NEEDED

Take some good brandy or nettles, one drachm of ginger, camphor, fishberry, herb and nasturtium, of each one drachm, of cloves one scruple, or rue toothwort, eyebalm so much as may be held between two fingers (one pinch). Bruise all these articles, and put into the brandy, and distill it in the sun, during the winter season 24 days in a warm room. Dip your finger therein and rub the eyelids therewith, morning and evening, this will keep the eyes clear, and make them strong without the use of spectacles.

TO RECOVER STOLEN GOODS

Mark well whence the thief left and by which door; from it cut three pieces of wood while pronouncing the three most sacred names; take these scraps of wood to a wagon, but in a noiseless manner, take a wheel off the wagon and insert the wood in the nave, again pronouncing the three holiest names, then drive the wheel backward and ejactulate: Thief, thief, return with the stolen article, thou shalt be compelled by the omniscience of God the Father, the Son and the Holy Spirit. God the Father calls thee back, God the Son turn thy footsteps that thou must return, God the Holy Spirit guide thee to retrace thy steps until thou again reachest this place. By dint of God's power thou must come back, by the wisdom of the Son of God thou shalt enjoy no peace nor rest till all the stolen things are returned to the rightful owner. By the grace of God the Holy Ghost, thou must run and leap, canst neither rest nor sleep till thou shalt arrive at that place where thou has committed the theft. God the Father bind thee, God the Son compel thee, God the Holy Ghost cause thee to return. The wheel, thou must not rapidly turn, or the soles of his feet may blister and burn, he will in pain and anguish cry, and ere you catch him, thus may die; Thou shalt come in the name of the Father, the Son and the Holy Spirit. Thief, thou must come. Thief thou must come. If thou art mightier, thief, thief, thief, than God and the Holy Trinity, then stay where thou art. The ten commandments force thee to observe not to steal, hence thou must return.

TO SECURE ONE'S SELF AGAINST ROBBERS WHILE TRAVELING

Speak three times: Two wicked eyes have overshadowed me, but three other eyes are overshadowing me too, the one of God, the Father, the other God the Son, the third of God the Holy Spirit, they watch my blood and flesh, my marrow and home, and all other large and small limbs, they shall be protected In the name of God.

ALSO FOR THE TOOTHACHE

St. Peter stood under an oak tree. Then spake our beloved Redeemer to Peter: Why art thou sad and weary? Peter replied: Why should I not feel sad and dread, since all the teeth decay in my head? Wherupon our Lord Jesus Christ spake unto Peter: Peter, hie to the cool and lonely nook, there runs a clear water in a mountain brook. Take water thereof in thy decaying' mouth, and spew it again into the running brook. This done three times in succession, and each time the three highest names pronounced. This repeat for three days in succession.

HOW TO MAKE ONE'S SELF AGREEABLE TO ALL

Carry a whoop's eye on your person. If you carry it in

front of your breast, all your enemies will become kind to you, and If you carry it in your purse you make a good bargain on all what you sell.

TO FASTEN A PERSON THAT HE MAY NOT ESCAPE

Take a needle wherewith the gown from a corpse had been sewed and put this needle into the foot prints of the person you seek to fasten. And never will that person, so treated, be able to get away.

TO HAVE GOOD LUCK IN PLAYING, AND HOW TO MAKE YOURSELF LIKED BY PEOPLE

Take the right thumb in your hand, and put the hand in your right hand pocket whenever a delinquent is executed, and thus you will secure good luck in playing and be liked by your fellow-men.

TO TRY IF A PERSON IS CHASTE

Sap of raddish squeezed into the hand will prove what you wish to know. If they do not fumble or grabble they are all right.

HOW TO CAUSE YOUR INTENDED WIFE TO LOVE YOU

Take feathers from a rooster's tail, press them three times into her hand. Probatum. Or: Take a turtle dove tongue into your mouth, talk to your friend agreeably, kiss her and she will love you so clearly that she cannot love another.

WHEN YOU WISH THAT YOUR SWEETHEART SHALL NOT DENY YOU

Take the turtle dove tongue into your mouth again and kiss her, and she will accept your suit. Or: Take salt, cheese and flour, mix it together, put it into her room, and she will have no rest until she sees you.

AN AMBROSE-STONE

Steal the eggs of a raven, boil them hard, lay them again into the nest and the raven will fly across the sea and bring a stone from abroad and lay it over the eggs and they will become at once soft again. If such a stone is wrapped up into a bay leaf and is given to a prisoner, that prisoner will be liberated at once. Whoever touches a door with such a stone, to him that door will be opened, and he who puts that stone into his mouth will understand the song of every bird.

WHEN AN ANIMAL IS STUPID

When an animal is stupid, when it runs around as if it had the rams, or when it carries the head upon one side, which signifies a sort of woe or pain, it may arise from heat and superfluous blood; hence it would be good to bleed such a beast three or four times, especially on a Friday. In all cases, however, an animal should suffer from such an ailment, pronounce the following grace three times over it, the first time stand upon the right side of the animal; the second time on its left side; the third time again upon the right side, and while saying the grace move constantly your hand over the back of the animal.

TO MAKE ONE'S SELF SHOT-PROOF

According to this formula, on the day of Peter and Paul, at vesper tide, there spring open waywort roots, of which hunters and men of the forest believe that he who carries them on his person cannot be hit or shot.

TO CATCH FISH

Take valerian, or cocculus Indicus, and make small cakes thereof with flour; throw these into the deep. As soon as a fish eats thereof it will become intoxicated, and float upon the surface.

TO BANISH ALL ROBBERS, MURDERERS, AND FOES

God be with you, brethren. Desist you thieves, robbers, murderers, waylayers and warriors in meekness, because we all have partaken of the rose colored blood of Jesus Christ. Your rifles, gun, and cannons be spiked, with the holy drops of our Redeemer's blood. All sabers and deadly weapons be closed, with the five wounds of our dear Master, Jesus Christ. Three roses are blooming on Jesus' heart. The first is kind, the other is mighty, the third represents God's strong will. Under 13 these,, ye thieves and murderers are become "still, as long as I will, and ye are banished, and your foul deeds have vanished.

TO CITE A WITCH

Take an earthen pot, not glazed, yarn spun by a girl not yet seven years old. Put the water of the bewitched animal into the pot, then take the egg of a black hen and some of the yarn and move the latter three times round the egg, and ejaculate in the three devils' names; after this put the egg into the water of the pot, seal the lid of the vessel tightly that no fumes may ooze therefrom, but observe that the head of the lid is below. "While setting the pot upon the fire, pronounce the following: Lucifer, devil, summon the sorcerer before the witch or me, in the three devils' name.

IN CASE ONE SUFFERS FROM A THEFT

If something is stolen from you, proceed also as stated above, take likewise water, draw it from a brook stream downward, and cut three splinters from the threshold over which the thief did run. The water must be drawn in the three names of the devil.

THAT NO WITCH MAY LEAVE A CHURCH

Purchase a pair of new shoes, grease them on Saturday with grease on the outer sole, then put them on and walk to the church, and no witch can find the way out of the church without you proceed before her.

ANOTHER WAY TO CAUSE RETURN OF STOLEN PROPERTY

Take three pieces of bread, three pinches of salt and three pieces of hog's lard, make a strong flame, put all the articles upon this fire, and say the following words, while keeping alone: I put bread, salt and lard for the thief upon the fire, for thy sin and temerity so dire. I place them upon thy lungs, liver and heart, that thou art troubled with terror and smart, a distress shall come over thee with dread as if thou wert to be smitten dead, all veins in thy body shall burst and break, and great havoc and trouble shall make, that thou shalt have no peace nor rest, till what thou hast stolen thou hast returned and brought all back from whence it were taken. Three times to recite and every time the three holiest names spoken.

TO OBTAIN MONEY

Take the eggs of a swallow, boil them, return them to the nest, and if the old swallow brings a root to the nest, take it, put it into your purse, and carry it in your pocket, and be happy.

TO OPEN LOCKS

Kill a green frog, expose it to the sun for three days, powder or pulverize it. A little of this powder put into a lock will open the same.

TO UNDERSTAND THE SONG OF BIRDS

Take the tongue of a vulture, lay it for three days and three nights in honey, afterward under your tongue, and thus you will understand all the songs of birds.

TO STOP THE BLEEDING OF A WOUND

Take a small bone of a human body and put into the

wound, and the blood will cease to flow.

HOW TO OBTAIN A GOOD MEMORY

Take the gall of a partridge, and with it grease the temples every month, and your memory will be like that of Mnemon.

TO MAKE A PERSON DISLIKE GAMBLING

Speak to an executioner, and get some wood of a whip wherewith he has beaten criminals, and flog the gambler with this upon his naked body, and never more thereafter will he gamble.

WHILE TRAVELING

Say every morning: Grant me, oh Lord, a good and pleasant hour, that all sick people may recover, and all distressed in body or mind, repose or grace may find, and guardian angel may over them hover; and all those captive and in bondage fettered, may have their conditions and troubles bettered; fo all good travelers on horse or foot, we wish a safe journey joyful and good, and good women in labor and toil a safe delivery and joy.

THAT NO PERSON WILL DENY ANYTHING TO YOU

Take a rooster, three years old, throw it into a new earthen pot, and pierce it through, then put it into an ant's hill, and let it remain until the ninth day thereafter, then take it out again and you will find in its head a white stone, which you must carry on your person, and then nobody will deny you anything.

GOLD ROOTS FOR THE TEETHING OF CHILDREN

When children are teething suspend gold roots around their necks, and they will get their teeth without pain. Such root, carried on your person, secures the wearer against all harm. Waywort heals heart woe and stomach pain. Whoever carries the roots on his person his eyes will be cured. Dog's dribbling and ailments leave and wane like the moon, its flowers heal those who suffer from too large a spleen or milt. Nasturtian roots powdered, and laid upon the eyes, give clear and brilliant eyes. The sap to drink will cure liver complaint; whoever carries the root on his person will be favored.

TALISMANS, CHARMS, SPELLS AND INCANTATIONS

Spells of such force no wizard grave
E'er framed in dark Thessalian cave,
Though his could this ocean dry,
And force the planets from the sky.

TALISMANS

In the whole circle of the occult sciences there is scarcely anything more obstruse or intricate than the mystical science of Talismans. The use of them has occasionally received much opposition from incredulous individuals; while on the other hand, it has stood the ground with firmness amidst the change of ages. Mourning rings, miniatures, lockets, mementoes, armorial bearings, and the "boast of heraldry," are but so many relics of Talismanic learning, Amongst mankind in general, there is much of talismanic belief; witness the avidity with which the caul of an infant is sought after to preserve from danger by water; as also the celebrated romance of "The Talisman," by Sir Walter Scott; the intense interest of which arises from the narration of a singular instance of the faith formerly reposed in Talismanic agency. It is now well known that when Napoleon went to Egypt he was then presented with a talisman by a learned eastern magician, the effect of which was to protect and defend him from sudden attacks, assassinations, and all manner of hurts from firearms.

TALISMAN FOR LOVE

This Talisman is said to he wonderfully efficacious in procuring success in amours and love adventures. It should be made or prepared when Venus, the planet of love, is the evening star. It should be made preferably of pure silver, but where that is not practicable, cut out the picture of the Talisman from this book, and paste it neatly in any suitable article, such as in a locket, back of a watch, or it may be pasted on a piece of round cardboard of equal size and worn over the heart or the left breast, or carried in the pocket as a Lucky Pocket Piece.

TALISMAN AGAINST ENEMIES

Where possible this Talisman should be cast of the purest grain tin, and during the increase of the moon. The characters are to be engraved on it also during the increase of the moon. Where this is not practicable, the illustration may be cut out of this book and placed in, say, a locket, and suspended about the neck, or worn on any part of the body, or it may be pasted on a piece of round cardboard of equal size and carried in the pocket. It should be kept from the sight of all but the wearer. Its effects are to give victory over enemies, protection against their machinations, and to inspire the wearer thereof with the most remarkable confidence

TALISMAN FOR WAR AND BATTLE

This Talisman bears on it the powerful words, and also the awful sign which were said to have been conveyed to the Emperor Constantine from heaven, in daylight, and in the presence of his whole army, and whereby he was victorious in battle. It should be made of highly tempered steel, but where not practicable, the illustration may be cut out of this book and placed in a locket or other suitable article, or simply pasted on a piece of cardboard of similar size. It should be tied around the sword-arm. An ancient manuscript says of this Talisman: "He that beareth this sign about him shall be helped in every need and necessity."

TALISMAN FOR DESTROYING INSECTS AND REPTILES

This Talisman is to be made, if possible, of iron, when the sun and moon enter the sign, Scorpio. It has been proved to be powerful in effect; so much so that no kind of venomous reptile or troublesome insect can come within some yards of the house or place in which it is. The manuscript from which the account of this Talisman is taken, cost a very large sum and a medical gentle nan to whom it belonged, affirms that he had himself proved its efficacy, for being at one time much annoyed with beetles, he made a talisman, according to instructions here given and screwed it to the floor, when these troublesome insects Immediately disappeared, but afterwards, when the servant removed it, through ignorance, they returned in great numbers; when he again nailed It to the floor, and they again disappeared! If impractical to have this Talisman specially made, the illustration may be cut out of this book and pasted on a piece of heavy tin or other metal, or even a stout piece of cardboard.

TO OVERCOME CHARMS AND EVIL INFLUENCE

Repeat reverently, and with sincere faith, the following words, and you shall be protected in the hour of danger: "Behold, God is my salvation; I will trust, and not be afraid, for the Lord Jehovah is my strength and my song; He also Is become my salvation. For the stars of heaven, and the constellations thereof, shall not give their light; the sun shall be darkened in his going forth, and the moon shall not cause her light to shine. And behold, at evening tide, trouble; and before the morning he is not; this is the portion of them that spoil us, and the lot of them that rob us."

CHARM AGAINST TROUBLE IN GENERAL

Repeat reverently, and with sincere faith, the following words, and you shall be protected in the hour of danger: "He shall deliver the six troubles, yea, in seven there shall no evil touch thee. "In famine he shall redeem thee from death, and in war from the power of the sword. And thou shalt know that thy tabernacles shall be in peace, and thou Shalt visit thy habitation and shalt not err."

CHARMS, OMENS, AND SIGNS

The use of charm and talisman is extensive, and a great percentage of the people have their pet "lucky piece" always with them. Magnetic lodestones are universally used to attract good fortune, love and happiness, likewise with various lucky images or idols. Belief in these lucky pieces extends back into history of thousands of years.

CLOUDS

Fleecy clouds indicate either a long wet or dry spell. Long streaky clouds denote fair weather. A halo around the moon is a. sign of rain. An uneven number of reports of lightning in quick succession is a sign of good luck. Thunder from a clear sky is also Indicative of good fortune.

PHYSICAL SIGNS AND OMENS

It is unlucky to see a new moon for the first time through a glass. A bee, flying in the house, should be retained for a few minutes as a prisoner to bring luck. Crickets in the house are considered a sign of luck, but a sign of illness if they leave without apparent reason. A sick person witnessing a shooting star will recover within the month. The howling of dogs denotes impending disaster. Robins are looked upon as messengers of good luck. To kill a moth hovering about a candle is to invite good luck. If a knife be dropped, accidently, so that the point penetrates the ground and stands upright, good luck will result. To spill salt on the table is considered unlucky. To counteract the spell, throw a pinch of the salt over the left shoulder. If your teakettle wings, it is a sign of happiness and contentment in your house. A spark on the wick of a candle means a letter will be received by the one who first sees it. To move into a new home on Friday is unlucky; however, Monday and Wednesday are particularly fortunate. A girl standing under a piece of mistletoe may be kissed by any man finding her there. Should the girl refuse the kiss, she invites bad luck. To put your clothes on the wrong way is a sign of good luck, if performed without intention. However, the clothes must be worn that way, else the luck changes. If you observe a shooting star, make a wish while it is still in motion, and the wish will come true. A rabbit running across your path is a sign of impending ill luck. The continual hooting of owls at night is an omen of ill-health. Should you wash your hands or face in water just used by another, be sure to first sprinkle a few drops on your head before emptying the vessel to avoid bad luck. Sunshine and the sneezing of a cat are said to be happy omens for brides. A creeping child will have better luck and be more fortunate in life than one that does not. Horseshoes are always considered lucky, and should be hung over the door of the house or barn. The horseshoe on the barn insures a good harvest. If you see a pin, pick it up, as it will bring you good luck; to let it lie is bad luck. Never relate a bad dream before breakfast, lest it come true. The new moon first seen over the right shoulder offers an opportunity for a wish to come true. To break a mirror is considered unlucky, and the person breaking the glass will have bad fortune for seven years. In Catholic countries a person who accidentally breaks a mirror, crosses himself and repeats, "May the Saints avert ill fortune." However, if a glass is wilfully and purposely broken and thrown away, it will have no effect on the person breaking the glass.

POPULAR SUPERSTITIONS

KNOCKING ON WOOD

The custom of knocking on wood to prevent ill luck is

perhaps the most prevalent custom in existence, and is performed by all classes of people, the world over. Its origin is attributed to the ancient religious rite of touching a crucifix when taking an oath. It is said that a president of the United States is accused of resorting to this strange custom.

THE EVIL EYE

Fear of being bewitched by the "evil eye" is very prevalent among the Latin races, and in this country the belief is widespread that certain persons, possessing power of the devil and supernatural agencies, can bewitch another by simply looking at him with hatred in the eyes, and thus cast a spell. Psychology teaches that it is possible to influence others with your mind, the expression and influence going from the eyes, however, this should not be termed as the "evil eye spell," which is in reality a myth. However, many people still cling to the belief and wear charms and amulets to counteract the bad influence of the evil eye. These charms really aid these people, as it changes the negative thoughts of their minds to positive ones. Perhaps the most popular amulet is a cross of jet, the belief being that it will split if looked upon by a person having evil intentions. In some parts of the world, the face of a new born child is gently brushed with a bough of pine to prevent any evil influences from attacking the child. The Hindus dies. Taken in food, it is good for cancer. When you catch a whoop, you will find a stone which you must put under the head of a sleeping person, and that person will be compelled to impart to you all secrets which he may know. If you carry a badger's foot with you, all your affairs will be fortunate, and you will not be perplexed nor err. Whoop eyes make a man benign. If you carry the eye with you, you will be in good repute by the authorities; and if you will carry the head no one will cheat you. If you carry the head of a crow upon your breast, all must love you who have dealings with you. When you catch a mole and put it into a pot, while it lives, and ignite sulphur, all moles will gather together. When you put a mole into an earthen pot, and boil the same, and with this water wash the hair, the hair will turn white. During the month of August take a swallow from its nest. In its stomach you will find a stone, which you may wrap into a linen handkerchief, hang under your left arm. It is a good thing against slanderers, and makes you agreeable among the people. A snail is said to have a starlet in its head, and when found it is good for one who is afflicted with kidney disease.

WHEN A PERSON HAS SPRAINED HIMSELF

Take juniper berries and hay flowers, bruise them and boil in good old wine. Apply as a poultice.

TO MAKE YOURSELF INVISIBLE

Pierce the right eye of a bat, and carry it with you, and you will be invisible.

TO PREVENT CHILDREN HAVING MEASLES FROM BECOMING BLIND

As soon as the children get sick from measles, hang on their necks the roots of purnellac, and your sorrows may cease. Probatum.

HOW TO DRAW OUT A THORN OR SPLINTER

Take carrots bruised with honey and make a powder thereof. Put over the injury; it will draw the substance out and soothe the pains.

WHEN LUNGS OF CATTLE SWELL

Take some sandstone, put it into a bake-oven till it becomes hot, then put it into a pail of fresh water. Let the cattle drink.

FOR THE ITCH OR SCAB

Take precipitate, lard and white hen's manure, make a lye therefrom and wash the skin therewith.

FOR OPEN SORES

Take hog's lard of the size of a bean, heat it; put the yolk of an egg and some saffron therein; stir it well and it will heal.

WHEN A PERSON HAS IMBIBED TOO MUCH

Take fungus of a linden tree, one-half quart of old wine, one-half quart of water, pour the latter on the fungus, let it draw for twenty-four hours and drink mornings, noons and evenings thereof, one teaspoonful.

SALVE FOR GOUTY LIMBS

Take dog's lard for five cents, oil of white fir tree cones five cents, olday for five cents, seal oil for five cents, a quart of lard in which all the others are rendered down, and the gouty limb anointed with the salve.

FOR COAGULATED BLOOD

Take five cents worth of nomo, make a plaster of it and put it on the injury once or twice.

TO DRIVE AWAY LICE

Fishberry and lard mixed together and the head anointed therewith.

A DRINK FOR HORSES

Watercresses, green juniper berries, hartshorn; Venetian soap. Of these make a beverage.

WHEN A GUN IS BEWITCHED

Take five cents worth of liquid amber, assafoetida, river water, and mix well together. With the mixture clean well, and the rag, with which the scouring was made, hang up in the smoke or put into a new made grave.

HOW TO KEEP WARM IN WINTER

Take nettlewort, garlic, pour lard into it and boil together. When hands and feet are greased with this ointment one will not feel cold.

FOR A WEAK HEAD

When a person has a weak head and is often absent-minded, take hold of an ant's hill, then put them in a bag, boil the same for six hours in a kettle of water. Draw this water upon bottles and distil it in the sun. With such water wash the weak and dull head. If the disease is very bad bathe the patient in this water. The blood of asses can be drunk. Decorate their children with beautiful jewels to confuse and antagonize the evil eye. Mohammedans hang articles from the ceiling over the cradle of their children to ward off evil influences, the key to the house being considered the most beneficial article.

THE BLACK CAT

As a rule, black cats are considered unlucky, but contrary to general belief, are supposed to bring good luck. However, to kill a black cat is unlucky and invites misfortune for a year. A black cat crossing your path denotes good luck, not bad. The meowing of a black cat at midnight is a bad omen. Various actions of cats are supposed to foretell good or unfortunate events.

COLOR SUPERSTITIONS

Color has a great influence on the mentality of individuals. Everyone is supposed to possess a color hue, and your color chart will correspond with that of your lucky star. Color rules the emotions as follows: Red governs love, affection and lust. Red is also the paramount advertising color, as it is the most attractive to the eye. Orange denotes simplicity and ignorance. Orange is the color of the god of marriage. Scarlet rules the emotion and anger, and a color to be avoided by virtuous people. Bright red, symbolistic of Are, represents power, courage and confidence. Yellow signifies glory and fortune to the ancients. Now it is interpreted as denoting infidelity, perfidy and shame. Brown denotes worldly knowledge and is a mark of distinction. Green, the color of springtime, is associated with youth and hope. * Black is the color of sadness, gloom and death, while white denotes all that is pure and desired.

LUCKY STONES

Birthstones are generally accepted as inducing fortunate occurences. Each stone is governed by a different month or Sign of the Zodiac. They are as follows: January — Gafnet. February — Amethyst. March — Bloodstone. April — Diamond. May — Emerald. June — Agate. July — Ruby. August — Sardonyx. September — Sapphire. October — Opal. November — Topaz. December — Turquoise. Not being contented with a lucky gem for each month, the ancient philosophers allotted a stone for each day of the week, as follows: Sunday — Ruby and chrysolite. Monday — Selenite, pearl and opal. Tuesday — Amethyst and bloodstone. Wednesday— Agate, jade and olivine. Thursday — Emerald and sapphire. Friday — Turquoise and lapis-lazuli. Saturday — Onyx.

HOW TO MAKE YOUR LOVER OR SWEETHEART COME

If a maid wishes to see her lover, let her take the following method: Prick the third or wedding finger of your left hand -with a sharp needle (beware a pin), and with the blood write your own and lover's name on a piece of clean writing paper, in as small a compass as you can, and encircle it with three round rings of the same crimson stream, fold it up, and exactly at the ninth hour of the evening bury it with your own hand in the earth, and tell no one. Your lover will hasten to you as soon as possible, and he will not be able to rest until he sees you, and if you have quarrelled to make it up. A young man may also try this charm, only instead of the wedding finger, let him pierce the left thumb.

FOLK-LORE OF PINS

Why, however, north country people are so persistent in their refusal to give one another a pin it is not easy to discover, as even they themselves cannot give the origin and reason of this superstition. When asked for a pin they invariably say, "You may take one, but mind, I do not give it." It may, perhaps, have some connection with the vulgar prejudice against giving a knife, or other sharp instrument, as mentioned by Gay in his "Shepherd's Week." But woe is me! such presents luckless prove, For knives, they tell me, always sever lope. — A supposition as popular now as in days gone by. Another fact associated with pins will doubtless interest those of the fair sex about to enter on the happy state of matrimony. Thus, it is still a prevalent belief in certain places that a bride, in removing her bridal robe and chaplet at the completion of the marriage ceremonies, must take special care to throw away every pin worn on this eventful day. Woe to the bride who keeps even one pin used -in the marriage toilet. Woe also to the bridesmaids if they retain any of them, as their chances of marriage will thereby be materially lessened, and anyhow they must give up all hope of being wedded before the following Whitsuntide. On the other hand, in Sussex on her return home from church the bride is often robbed of all the pins about her dress by her single friends present, from the belief that whoever possesses one of them will be married in the course of a year. Much excitement and amusement are occasionally caused by the youthful competitors for this supposed charm, and the bride herself is not infrequently the victim of rather rough treatment.

MAGICAL PROPERTIES OF PINS

Among the magical properties of pins we may mention their supposed efficacy in the cure of certain disease. Thus, in Alabama, in the case of warts, the patient is taken to an ash tree, where a pin is first stuck into the bark, and withdrawn; a wart is transfixed with it till he feels pain, and then the pin is again pushed into the tree. Every wart entirely disappears. A few years ago we are told that some trees might be seen thickly studded with pins, each the index of a cured wart. In connection with this superstition there is a well known couplet: Ashen tree, ashen tree. Pray buy these warts of me. In place of a pin, a nail driven into an oak is reported to cure toothache. A "Virginia remedy consists in rubbing the warts with a snail, after it has been pierced with a pin as many times as there are warts. As the snail by degrees withers away, so it is believed that the wart, impregnated with its matter, will do the same. It has been pointed out that most of the charms of this kind are of the nature of a sacrifice, the warts being transferred to a substitute.

DREAMS THAT COME TRUE

A poor peasant, dwelling in the vicinity of Rheims, saw, one night, during his slumbers, a young man, who, taking him by the hand, conducted him to the base of an old wall, where, after designating a huge stone recommending him to raise it up on the morrow, he suddenly vanished. The peasant followed his advice, and found the stone indicated in his dream, which upon being displaced, and revealed a vase filled with golden coins — enriching the dreamer and his family. Gassius of Parma, who had espoused the cause of Mark Antony, fled to Athens after the battle of Actium. While sleeping in his apartments there, he saw a man enter his chamber, an individual with dark complexion and dishevelled hair, very tall and stout. Cassius demanded who he was; to which the phantom replied, "I am your evil genius." The dreamer arose in affright, and seeing no one present, summoned his slaves, inquiring if any among them had seen a stranger enter the apartment. An examination showed the doors of the house to have been firmly closed, so that it was impossible for anyone to enter. Cassius, persuaded that he had been the victim of some chimerical illusion, again went to sleep, but the same vision presented itself a second time, addressing him with the same words. Cassius, troubled arose from his couch and summoned lights. At early daybreak he was assassinated by order of the Emperor Augustus.

MURDER REVEALED

Two Arcadian friends, journeying together, arrived at Megara, at which place the one took lodgings at the house of a friends, while his companion put up at a public tavern. The traveler lodging at his friend's, was visited in a dream by his comrade, who supplicated him to come extricate him from a trap set for him by the innkeeper. He awoke suddenly, arose, dressed and hastened towards the tavern, when an afterthought compelled him to return, and he again undressed and went to sleep. Again his comrade presented himself, but this time covered with blood, and beseeching: him to avenge his murder. The phantom informed his fellow traveler that he had been treacherously assassinated by the tavern keeper, and his body concealed beneath a dunghill outside the city gates. Terrified at this second apparition, the Arcadian hesitated no longer, but going to the place designated, he discovered his friend's corpse, and was therefore enabled to bring the murderer to justice.

LUCKY DREAMS

A tradesman of Paris, sleeping in bed with his wife, dreamed that he heard a voice exclaiming to him: "I have now finished forty years, seven months, and twenty-nine days of labor and I am happy." The wife, sleeping by her husband's side, had the same dream, and upon awakening in the morning went forth, and without mentioning the occurrence, procured a lottery ticket bearing the numbers 40-729. The same day the numbers came out, and the tradesman lamented his indiscretion in not taking the advice of his nocturnal visitor. His sorrow was turned into joy when he learned that his wife, profiting by her dream, had drawn the grand prize in the Royal Lottery. An old lady of Paris was in the habit of encouraging her niece by promises of wealth, which she never fulfilled; extenuating her procrastination from year to year by recourse of ingenious expedients, and she finally died. Shortly after her decease, the aunt appeared during the night-time and instructed her niece to remove the center tile of their hearth, where she would discover the oft-promised treasure. The young girl obeyed the injunction, but discovered in the cavity nothing save a heap of cinders. In vexation of spirit, the niece railed vehemently against the duplicity of a relative deceiving her after death. On the following night, however, the phantom again appeared, and without saying a word, designated four numbers apparently on the wall. Although placing little reliance upon 19 the injunction which she conceived to relate to a lottery (then the town talk), the niece resolved to try her luck, especially as the ticket offered for her purchase by the dealer bore the same numbers designated by the apparition.

Subsequently, these numbers came out in the order indicated, and the girl came into possession of four hundred thousand francs.

DIONYSIUS' VISION

Dionysius, of Syracuse, while lying one night upon his couch, awake and contemplative, heard a loud noise, and arose to ascertain the cause of it. He perceived at the end of the gallery a woman of gigantic stature, as hideous in countenance as one of the Furies, engaged in sweeping the mansion with a gigantic broom. In terror and affright, the tyrant summoned his friends and caused them to spend the remainder of the night with him. But the specter re-appeared no more. Two days after this vision, the son of Dionysius fell from a window and was killed, and before a week had elapsed his entire family was destroyed, and thus, observes the historian Leloyer, it can be justly said that Dionysius and his race were swept off the face of the earth in the same manner in which the Fury, the avenging genius of Syracure, had been seen to sweep out the palace.

OBSERVATIONS CONCERNING THE EYES

Spots in the eyes are of two sorts; either they appear in the white of the eye (and this shows the sudden redundancy of melancholy as appears in such as are near death), or when the eyes are maculated with black spots proceeding from habitual melancholy, and is a certain index of the afflicting passions of the mind; or else the eyes are masculated with spots like the grain of millet, or quadrangle; and if divers various colors, as fiery, red, azure, or of a rainbow color, all of which indicates mad, wild, cruel, and the worst of conditions; from whence we may pronounce most horrid events, and unnatural death. The following additional observations concerning eyes will be found interesting and useful: 1. Great eyes denote a slothful, bold and lying person, of a rustic and coarse mind. 2. Byes deep in the head denote a great mind, yet full of doubts, but generous and friendly, and if they are blue or gray, they signify great knowledge; if they are of a greenish cast they intermix malice, injury and envy, and if red, they are of the nature of the cat. 3. Eminent and apparent eyes of a wall color, denote a simple, foolish, and prodigal person. 4. Sharp and piercing eyes, that decline the eyebrows, denote a deceiver, and a secret and lawless person. 5. Little eyes, like those of a mole or pig, denote a weak understanding, and easily to be imposed on. G. Beware of squint eyes, for out of one hundred, you will not find two faithful; for the possessor will be sly, cunning, and insinuating. It is very ill luck to meet a squinting person, and from long experience, I would wish that a person going out on business or any great expectations, meeting a squinting person of either sex, would return home and defer their business till another day, if they wish for success. 7. Eyes that move slowly, and look sleepy, denote an unfaithful, slothful, and riotous person. 8. The worst of all the eyes are the yellowish or citron; beware of them, for the possessor is a dangerous person if you are in his power. 9. Beware also of them who, when they awake, twinkle their eyes, for they are double minded. If it is a woman that does so with her left eye, trust her not as to the faithfulness of her love, and have an eye upon her actions. 10. A child who has a blue vein across her nose, between the eyes, is a general sign that it will not live long, but if it survives its infancy, it will be very passionate, and a great trouble to its family. But you seldom will find deceit where the eye looks with a modest confidence, not staring you out of countenance, nor averting as if detected of a crime; but when in business, love, or friendship, there appears a tender firmness, the consclousnes of the integrity of the heart and conduct are thereby expressed.

SIGNS TAKEN FROM PARTS OF THE EYES

1. The angle of the eyes over long, indicates malevolent condition. 2. The angles being short, show a laudable nature; if the angles near the nose are fleshy, they denote hot constitution and improbity. 3. The balls of the eyes are equal, declare justice — unequal, the contrary. 4. The circles in the eyes of various colors and dry, denote fraudulency and vanity; but moist, denote fortitude, prudence and eloquence. 5. The lower circle green, and the upper black, are sure signs of a deceiver, and fraudulent person. 6. Eyes of moderate bigness, clear and shining, are signs of an ingenious, noble, generous and honest mind.

THE SILENT LANGUAGE

By motion of the hands. This art is performed by the twenty-four letters of the hand and fingers, which you must learn, and then you must spell the words you intend your friend should know; the letters are very easily learned, and as easily remembered. I have taught several persons in less than half an hour. You must understand that most of the letters are upon the left hand, and made with the fin20 gers of your right hand upon your left hand; the forefinger of your right hand you point to every letter; but some times that and the two next fingers make several letters, as you will see. The vowels are very easy to remember, they being the tops or ends of your five fingers upon your left hand, and Y is the table or palm of your hand, thus:
The end of the top of the thumb is A
The end of the fore finger is E
The end of the middle finger is I
The end of the ring finger is O
The end of the little finger is U
The table on the palm of the hand is Y
One finger on the left thumb is B
Two fingers upon the left thumb is C
Three fingers upon the left thumb D
Your two fingers laid together F
Thumb your fists together G
Stroke the palm of both hands together H
Your fore finger upon the left wrist K
One finger on the back of the left hand L
Three fingers on the back of your left hand is M
Two fingers on the back of the left hand N
Clench your left hand, or fist P
Clench your right hand Q

Link your little fingers together R
The backs of your hands together S
The end of your fore finger to the middle joint of the other fore finger T
Two fingers upon the little finger of left hand W
Two fore fingers across X
Give two snaps with your fingers Z

Practice it but a few times over, and you will soon be perfect; several motions represent the likeness of the letters; as, one finger at the back of your hands is like I, two fingers like N, three is like M. The fore finger to the middle joint of the other fore finger is like T; two fingers across is like X; likewise B, C, D, is very easily remembered, one finger on the left thumb is B, two fingers C, three fingers D. So the rest are soon learned, and as easy to remember. But you must always remember to give a snap with your finger between every word, that your friend may distinguish one word from another. If you are in company, and think some one in company understands you, that you would not have, it is easy for you to change the vowels to some other part of the hand, and then none but your friend that knows it can understand you. Suppose you would say to your mistress, when she is in a great company, "Madam, I am your humble servant." Lay three fingers on the back of your hand. M
Put your finger to the end of your thumb A Three fingers upon your left thumb D
Your finger again to your thumb A
Three fingers again to back of your hand M
And give snap with your fingers, for the sign the word is spelled. Then point to end of your middle finger I
Then snap your fingers. Then point to the end of your

thumb A
Three fingers on the back of your hand M
Then snap your fingers. Then point to the palm of your left hand Y
Then point to the end of your ring finger O
Then point to the end of your little finger U
Then link your little fingers together R Then snap your fingers. Stroke the palms of your hands together H
Point to the end your little finger U
Put three fingers on the back of your hand M
One finger on the thumb B
One finger on the back of your hand L
Point to the end of your fore finger E
Then snap your fingers. Put the backs of your hands together S
Point to the end of your fore finger E
Link your little fingers together R
Point to the end of your little finger V
Point to the end of the thumb A
Lay two fingers on the back of your hand N
Point fore finger to middle joint of other finger. T

Then snap your fingers.

A FIGURE HAND

You ' must make an exchange and place these figures in the place:

aeiouytnsr
1234567890

And then your alphabet will run thus:
lbcd2fgh3km84pqo976wy62

Columbia, Columbia, to glory arise.C415mb31, C415mb31, 74 gl 40y 10392 You will find a great many words nothing but figures, and there is scarce any word, great or small, but has the greatest part figures. It is so plain to be learned that I need not give you any further instructions, but only to practice the ten figures instead of letters. The other hand is performed by exchanging of more letters, one for the other. a e i o u y t n s r When you are to write A, you must write Y, when you are to write Y, you must write A; and so on of all the rest. As for example, suppose you would say, "Sir, I am your humble servant," it is thus: Onu, n ym asru hrm, bit Oturyie This appears like another language, and puzzles the greatest wits, and with a little practice is soon learned, by reason there are but ten letters you are to learn for the other, your alphabet will be thus: abedefghoj klmnopqrstuvwxyz ybcdtfguhklmispQuoervwxai) I shall not proceed any further, because this is sufficient, but let the reader practice what is here shown him, and he may soon learn the whole art.

HOW TO WRITE LOVE LETTERS SECRETLY

To write love letters secretly, so that they shall not be discovered, take a sheet of white paper and double it In the middle, and cut holes through both the half sheets; let the holes be cut like a pane of glass, or other forms that you may fancy; then with a pin, prick two little holes at each end and cut your paper in two halves; give one half to your friend to whom you intend to write, lay your cut paper upon a half sheet of writing paper, and stick two pins in these holes that it stir not; then through these holes that you did cut, write your mind to your friend. When you have done, take off your paper holes again, and then write some other idle words both before and after your lines but if they were written to make some little sense, it would carry the less suspicion; then seal it up and send it. When your friend hath received it, he must lay his paper on the same, putting pins into the pin holes, and then he can read nothing but your mind that you write, for all the rest of the lines are covered. Another. — Write what you please of a letter on one side of a sheet of letter paper with common ink, then turn your paper, and write on the other side with milk, that which would have secret, and let it dry, but this must be written with a clean pen. Now when you would read it you must hold that Bide which is written with ink to the fire, and the milky letters will then show bluish on the other side.

THE WAY TO GET RICH AND LIVE HAPPY IN THE MARRIAGE STATE

"There is a tide in the affairs of men, which, taken at the flood, leads on to fortune." He that by the plow would thrive. Himself must either hold or drive. For age and want save while you may. No morning's sun lasts a whole day. Get what you can, and what you get, hold: 'Tis a stone that will turn all your lead to gold. Therefore he ruled by me, I pray; Save something for a rainy day. Remember, that time is money; for he that can earn $2.50 a day at his labor, and goes abroad or sits idle at home one-half of that day, though he spend but 10 cents during his diversion or idleness, he ought not to reckon that the only expense; he hath really wasted, or, rather, thrown away $1.00 besides. Remember, that credit is money. If a man let his money lay in my hands after it is due, because he has a good opinion of my credit, he gives me the interest, or so much as I can make of the money duringthat time. This amounts to a very considerable sum, where a man has large credit, and also makes good use of it. Remember, that money is of a prolific or multiplying nature. Money will produce money, and its offspring will produce more; and so $1.25 turned is $1.50; being turned again is $1.75; and so on, till it becomes a hundred dollars, and, the more there is of it, the more it will produce on every turning, so that the profits rise quicker and Quicker, and he who throws away $1 destroys all that it might have produced, even some scores of dollars. Remember this proverb: that the good paymaster is lord of another man's purse; for he - who is known to pay punctually and exactly to the time he promises, may, at any time, and on any occasion, raise all the money his friends can spare. This is sometimes of great use, next to industry and frugality. Nothing can contribute more to the raising of a man in the world than punctuality in all his dealings. Therefore, never keep borrowed money one single hour -beyond the time promised, lest the disappointment should shut up your friend's purse forever, aa the most trifling actions that affect a man's credit ought always to be avoided. The sound of the hammer at five o'clock in the morning, or at nine at night, being heard by a creditor, makes him easy six months longer; but, if he sees you at a gaming table, or hears your voice in a tavern when you should be at work, he sends for his money the very next day, and demands it before it is convenient for you to pay him. Beware of thinking all your own that you possess, and of living accordingly. This is a mistake that many people of credit fall into; but, in order to prevent this, always keep an exact daily account of both your expenses, and also of your daily income and profits; for, if you will only just take the trouble at first to enumerate particulars, you will discover unto you how wonderfully small trifling expenses mount up to a large sum; by Which you will also discern what might have been, and also what may for the future be saved without causing any great inconvenience. In short, the way to obtain riches, if you desire it, is as plain as the way to market, which depends chiefly oh two things, viz.: industry and frugality. And take care that you - waste neither time nor money but daily make the best use of both. If you take care of the hours and days, the weeks, months and years will also take care of themselves. I have always found, by constant experience, that any business, being first well contrived, is more than half done — for a sleeping fox catches no poultry. There will be sleep enough in the grave; and, also that lost time is but seldom found again, for that which we generally call time enough always proves little enough; for sloth makes things difficult, while industry makes them easy. He that rises late must trot hard all day, and shall scarce overtake his business at night — for laziness travels so slow that poverty soon overtakes him. Drive your business, but let not that drive you; for early to bed and early to rise is the way to become healthy, wealthy and wise. Industry need not want, -while he -who lives on a vain hope will do fasting; for we find that there is nothing to be done or accomplished under the sun without labor. He that hath a trade hath an estate, and he that hath a profession hath on office and profit -with honor, but then the trade must be worked at, and the profession well followed, or they will not enable you to pay rent and taxes; for, at the working man's house, hunger looks in, but dares not enter — for industry pays debts, while despair increases them. Diligence is the mother of good luck. As Solomon said, "The diligent hand maketh rich, while he that dealeth with a slack hand becometh poor," for God gives all things to industry. Then plow deep while sluggards sleep, and you shall have plenty, while others have reason to complain of hard times. Therefore, keep working -while it is called today, for you know not how much you may be hindered tomorrow; and never that business to be done tomorrow which you can do today; for, since you are not sure of a single hour, throw not that away. How many are there who live daily by their wits, and who often break for want of a stock In hand, while industry gives comfort, plenty and respect. Keep your shop well and then your shop will keep you. For it sometimes happens that the eye of a master "will do more work than both his hands, and more especially if his head be any reasonable length; for the want of care generally does more damage than the want of knowledge. If you do not watch your workmen, you may just as well leave them your purse open; for the trusting too much to the care of others has completely ruined many a man. Therefore, if you would be wealthy, think of being careful and saving; for "Women, wine, game, and deceit, Make the wealth small and the wants great."

OMENS

Omens, as signs that may be good or bad, resemble dreams in this, that they bring before us signals that we ourselves do not seek, and convey warnings that are of much significance to those who can read them right.

VALUE OF OMENS

In olden days, when superstition had a strong hold upon the minds of men, the abuse of this branch of Occultism led to much needless misery; but now that the clear light of science has scattered so many of the mists of mere superstition, we can set aside the more trivial accidents of life, which were looked upon with undue alarm, and cease to torment ourselves at every turn with groundless fears and nervous fancies, while we still believe that many secrets of Nature have been solved to which we should give earnest heed. Thus, while we may avoid walking under a ladder as much because a brick dislodged from above may fall upon our head, as from any dread of bad luck to follow, we do not doubt that there are many omens of more serious import to which we should attend.

SECOND SIGHT

Foremost among such grave omens, and nearest to the kindred realm of dreams, is that indication of future events which comes by which is known as Second Sight. A few years before his death Doctor Johnson visited places in Scotland where evidences of this mysterious faculty were frequent, for the special purpose of inquiring into the subject; and the following extracts from his account of it are full of interest: "Second sight," he says, "is an impression made either by the mind upon the eye, or upon the eye by the mind, by which things distant or future are perceived and seen as. if they were present. A man on a journey, far from home, falls from his horse; another, who is perhaps at work about the house, sees him bleeding on the ground, commonly with the landscape of the place where the accident befalls him. Another seer, driving home his cattle, or wandering in idleness, or musing in the sunshine, is suddenly surprised by the appearance of a bridal ceremony, or a funeral procession. Things distant are seen at the instant when they happen. The appearances have no dependence upon choice; they cannot be summoned, detained or recalled. The impression is sudden, and the effect often painful. I do not find it to be true that nothing is presented to the Second Sight but phantoms of evil. Good seems to have the same proportion in these visionary scenes as it has in real life. That they should often see death is to be expected, because death is frequent and important." According to Martin, an early writer on this subject, it is possible to some extent to classify these visions, and so to determine the time between the sight and the event. If an object was seen early in the morning, the event would take place in a few hours; if at noon, the same day; if at night, it would be fulfilled weeks, months, and sometimes years afterwards. The appearance of a shroud was a certain sign of death; if it was not drawn above the middle of the body, a delay of a year might be hoped for, but if it ascended high towards the head the mortal hour was close at hand. "The vision makes such a lively impression upon the Seers," says Martin, "that they neither see nor think of anything else as long as the vision continues; their eyelids are uplifted, and their eyes are staring so long as the sight can be seen."

NIGHT OMENS

Many methods have long been in use for discovering what the future holds in store in matters of love and marriage. If young people would dream of their lovers, let them secure a piece of the first cut of a "groaning cheese," a cheese made at the birth of a child in any family, and place it under their pillow. If this should fail "let them take a piece of cake made on a similar occasion, and known as "dreaming bread." Each inquirer must place this in the foot of the left stocking, and throw it over the right shoulder, and then retire to' bed backwards, and in perfect silence. If she falls asleep before midnight her future partner will appear in her dream. Yet another method is for anxious maidens to write their names on slips of paper at twelve o'clock, and to burn these; then to gather the ashes carefully, and lay them, closely wrapped in paper, upon a looking-glass marked with a cross under their pillows. This should make them dream of their loves.

SALT-SPILLING

The spilling of salt is reckoned to presage calamity, and particularly domestic strife. To avert this it is customary to fling a pinch of salt over the left shoulder. A writer on this subject says: "To scatter salt by overturning the salt-cellar is very unlucky, and portends a quarrel with a friend, a broken bone, or other bodily misfortune. This may be averted by throwing a small quantity over the head." Leonardo da Vinci, in his picture of The Last Supper, has represented the traitor Judas overturning the salt — a dark and ominous foreshadowing of the betrayal of his Master. Salt has long been esteemed a symbol of friendship, probably because it is considered incorruptible, but in the North it is thought unlucky to put it on another person's plate. Hence the saying — "Help me to salt, Help me to sorrow;" but any evil consequences may be averted by a second helping. Such are some of the principal omens which claim credence from all who understand "that there are more things in heaven and earth than are dreamed of in our philosophy," and there are many others to which we should give heed, even though some of them seem to be of little moment.

A STRING OF OMENS

The following are gathered from reliable sources; and are commended to the consideration of those who have "ears to hear." Birthdays. — An old rhyme says of our birthdays: "Sunday's child is full of grace, Monday's child is full in the face, Tuesday's child is solemn and sad, Wednesday's child is merry and glad, Thursday's child is inclined to thieving, Friday's child Is free in giving, Saturday's child works hard for his living." Another version of this runs thus: "Monday's child is fair of face, Tuesday's child is full of grace, Wednesday's child is full of woe, Thursday's child has far to go, Friday's child is loving and giving, Saturday's child works hard for its living; But a child that is born on the Sabbath day Is handsome and wise, and loving and gay." Clothes. — If you put on any of your garments inside out, be careful not to alter them, as by so doing you will incur bad luck. Crickets. — Do not on any account disturb a cricket in your house. Its presence is an omen of prosperity, and foretells money that is coming to you. Death watch. — If you hear a clinking sound in the wall of your house caused by the little insect commonly called the death-watch, regard it as a presage of some discomfort, but not necessarily of a death. Ears. — If your right ear tingles, some one is speaking well of you; if your left ear, then ill is spoken. If you run through the list of your friends and acquaintances, the tingling will cease as you name the person who is speaking of you. Knife or Fork. — If a knife, or fork, or a pair of scissors falls from your hand and sticks in the floor, it is a certain sign that visitors are coming to call upon you. Lady-birds. — A lady-bird is of similar omen. Magpies. — A single magpie seen out of doors portends bad luck; two tell of good fortune; three indicate a wedding, and four a birth. Folk in the northern counties say: "One for anger, two for mirth, Three for a wedding, four for a birth." Marriage. — A girl should never be married in colors. A widow should not marry in white. Among many happy omens for brides are sunshine, and the sneezing of a cat. Martins. — Martins nesting under your eaves bring good luck if undisturbed. May. — The month of May has been considered an unlucky time for marriages. Ovid in his "Fasti" declares this time to be unpropitious for the weddings of either widows or maidens, and the modern warning runs — "Marry in May, and you'll rue the day." Nails. — There is a time for everything, and the following quaint lines tell us when we should cut our nails— "A man had better ne'er been born Than have his nails on a Sunday shorn. Cut them on Monday, cut them for health ; Cut them on Tuesday, cut them for wealth; Cut them on Wednesday, cut them for news; 24 Cut them on Thursday for a pair of new shoes; Cut them on Friday, cut them for sorrow; Cut them on Saturday, see your sweetheart tomorrow." New Moon. — A new moon on Monday is a certain sign of fair weather and good luck. If you see a new moon for the first time over your right shoulder, and form a wish, you may expect it to be realized. New Year. — When first you see or eat anything new in the New Year, before speaking have a silent wish, and say some poet's name distinctly, otherwise your wishing will be vain. Nightingale. — It is a happy omen for lovers to hear the nightingale before the cuckoo. In his "Sonnet to the Nightingale" Milton says — "Thy liquid notes that close the eve of day, First heard before the swallow cuckoo's bill, Portend success in love." Owls. — The continuous hooting of owls in your trees is said to be an omen of ill-health. Pigs. — If you meet a sow coming toward you, it is an excellent omen; but should she turn from you, the luck is lost. Rabbits. — A rabbit running across your path is an unfavorable sign. Shoes. — 'It is considered unlucky to put on your left shoe first. Singing. — If you sing before breakfast you may expect bad news and sorrow before night. Sparks. — A red spark on the wick of a candle signifies a letter coming to the person who sees it first. Spiders. — Long-legged spiders are harbingers of good fortune. A small red spider — called sometimes a money spinner — running over you, is a sign of money coming to you. Do not in any way disturb it. Stars. — If you see a shooting star, and are quick enough to form a wish before it has vanished, you may be sure that your desires will come to pass. Stones or Pips. — If you have a number of fruit stones or pips on your plate, think of a wish, and then count the stones. If they are even, the omen is favorable; if odd, it is the reverse. Throwing Old Shoes. — The common custom of throwing an old shoe after a bride has a deeper meaning than the belief that it will bring good luck. It was originally the symbol of renunciation of authority over x her by her father or guardian, and its transference to her husband. This evidence of a change of ownership is of very ancient date, and traces of it are to be found in the Books of Ruth and Deuteronomy. Washing. — If you wash your hands in the water which some other person has just used, you should first make the sign of the cross over the water. If you neglect this precaution there Will be a quarrel between you. Weather and Bees. — Bees are weather-wise, and do not wander far from their hive if storms are at hand.

HOW TO BE A SPIRIT MEDIUM

The spirit-circle is the assembling together of a given number of persons for the purpose of seeking communion with the spirits that have passed away from earth into the higher world of souls. The chief advantage of such an assembly is the mutual impartation and reception of the combined magnetisms of the assemblage. These in combination form a force stronger than that of an isolated subject; first enabling the spirits to commune with greater power; next, developing the latent gifts of mediumship in such members of the circle as are thus endowed; and, finally, promoting that harmonious and social spirit of fraternal intercourse which is one of the especial aims of the spirits' mission. The first conditions to be observed relate to the persons who compose the circle. These should be, as far as possible, of opposite temperaments, as positive and negative in disposition, whether male or female; also of moral characters, pure minds, and not marked by repulsive points of either physical or mental condition. The physical temperaments should contrast with each other; but no person suffering from a decidedly chronic disease, or of a very debilitated physique, should be present at any circle unless it is formed expressly for healing purposes. I would recommend that the number of the circle never be less than three nor more than twelve. The use growing out of the association of differing temperaments is to form a battery on the principles of electricity or galvanism, composed of positive and negative elements, the sum of which should be unequal. No person of a very strongly positive temperament or disposition should be present, as any magnetic spheres emanating from the circle will overpower that of the spirits, who must always be positive to the circle in order to produce phenomena. It is not desirable to have more than two already well-developed mediums in a circle, as mediums always absorb the magnetism of the rest of the party; hence, when there are too many present, the force, being divided, cannot operate successfully with any. Of Temperature. — Never let the apartment be overheated, or even close. As an unusual amount of magnetism is liberated at a circle, the room is always warmer than it is ordinarily, and should be well ventilated. Avoid strong light, which, by producing excessive motion in the atmosphere, disturbs the manifestations. A very subdued light is the most favorable for any manifestations of a magnetic character, especially for spiritual magnetism. Of the Positions to Be Observed. — If the circle is one which meets another periodically, and is composed of the same persons, let them occupy the same seats (unless changed under spiritual direction), and sit (as the most favorable of all positions) around a table, their hands laid on it, with palms downward. It is believed that the wood, when charged, becomes a conductor, without the necessity of touching or holding hands. I should always suggest the propriety of employing a table as a conductor, especially as all tables in a household use are more or less magnetically charged already. If flowers and fruit are in the room, see that they are just freshly gathered, otherwise remove them; also avoid sitting in a room with many minerals, metals, or glasses, as these all injuriously effect sensitives, of whom mediums are the type. I recommend the seance to be opened either with prayer or music, vocal or instrumental; after which subdued, quiet and harmonizing conversation is better than wearisome silence; but let the conversation be always directed toward the purpose of the gathering, and never sink into discussion, or rise to emphasis; let it be gentle, quiet, and spiritual, until phenomena begin to be manifest. Always have a slate, or pen, pencil and paper on the table, so as not to be obliged to rise to procure them. Especially avoid all entering or leaving the room, moving about, irrelevant conversation or disturbances within or without the circle-room, after the seance has been once commenced. The spirits are far more punctual to seasons, faithful to promise and periodical in action than mortals. Endeavor, then, to fix your circle at a convenient hour, when you will be least interrupted, and do not fail in your appointments. Do not admit unpunctual late comers; nor, if possible, suffer the air of the room to be disturbed in any way after the sitting commences. Nothing but necessity, indisposition, or impressions (to be hereafter described) should warrant the least disturbance of the sitting, which should never exceed two hours, unless an extension of time be solicited of the spirits. Let the seance always extend to one hour, even if no results are obtained; it sometimes requires all that time for spirits to form their battery of the materials furnished. Let it be also remembered that all circles are experimental; hence no one should be discouraged if phenomena are not produced after the first few sittings. Stay with the same circle for six sittings; if no phemonena are then produced (provided all the above conditions are observed) you may be sure you are not rightly assimilated to each other; you do not form the requisite combinations, or neutralize each other. In that case, break up, and let that circle of members meet with other persons; that is, change one, two, or three persons of your circle for others, and so on until you succeed. A well developed test-medium may sit without injury for any person of any description of character or temperament; but a circle sitting for mutual development should never admit persons addicted to bad habits, criminals, sensualists, strongly positive persons of any kind, whether rude, skeptical, violent-tempered, or dogmatical. An humble, candid, inquiring spirit, unprejudiced, and receptive of truth, is the only frame of mind in which to sit for phenomena, the delicate magnetism of which is shaped, tempered, and made or marred as much by mental as physical conditions. When once any of the circle can communicate freely and conclusively with the spirits, the spirits can and will take charge of and regulate the future movements of the circle. Of Impressions. — Impressions are the voices of spirits speaking to our spirits, or else the admonitions of the spirit within us, and should always be respected and followed out, unless (which is very rare) suggestive of actual wrong in act or word. At the opening of the circle, one or more of the members are often impressed to change seats with others; one or more impressed with the desire to withdraw, or a strong feeling of repulsion to some member of the circle, makes it painful to remain there. Let any or all of these impressions be faithfully regarded, and, at commencing, pledge to each other the promise that no offense shall be taken by following out impressions. If a strong impression to write, speak, sing, dance, or gesticulate, possesses any mind present, follow it out faithfully. It has a meaning, if you cannot at first realize it. Never feel hurt in your own person, nor ridicule your neighbors, for any failure to express, or at first discover the meaning of the spirits impressing you. Spirit control is often deficient, and at first almost always imperfect. But by often yielding to it, your organism becomes more flexible, and the spirit more experienced; and practice in control is absolutely necessary for spirits as well as mortals. If dark and evil disposed spirits manifest to you, never drive them away, but always strive to elevate them, and treat them as you would mortals under similar circumstances. Do not always attribute false hoods to lying spirits or deceiving: mediums. Many mistakes occur in the communion of which you cannot always be aware. Strive in truth, but rebuke error gently; and do not always attribute it to design, but rather to mistake in so difficult and so experimental a stage of the communion as mortals at present enjoy the spirits. Unless strictly charged by spirits to do otherwise, do not continue to hold sittings with the same parties for more than a twelvemonth. After that time, if not before, fresh elements of magnetism are absolutely essential. Some of the original circle should withdraw and others take their place. All persons are subject to spirit influence and spirit guidance and control, but not all can so externalize this power as to use it consciously or be what is significantly called a medium; and finally, let it be remembered, that except in the case of trance-speakers no medium can ever hope to exercise successfully his or her gift in a large or promiscuous assembly; while trance speakers, no less than mediums for any other gift, can never be influenced by spirits far beyond their own normal capacity in the matter of the intelligence rendered; the magnetism of the spirit and the spirit-circle being but a quickening fire, which inspires the brain, stimulates the faculties, and, like a hot-house process on plants, forces in abnormal prominence dormant or latent powers of mind, but creates nothing. Even in the case of merely automatic speakers, writers, aping, tipping, and other forms of test mediums, the intelligence or idea of the spirit is always measurably shaped by the capacity idiosyncrasies of the medium. All spirit power is thus limited to expression by organism through Which it works; and spirits may control, inspire, and influence the human mind, but do not change or recreate it.

SECRET METHOD OF MESMERISM

HOW TO HYPNOTIZE

The method used to bring about the hypnotic conditions consists essentially in an imitation of the process of ordinary sleep, by means of verbal suggestion. Thus we actually bring sleep into existence by acting upon the imagination through action and speech. The skill of the operator consists in making the subject believe he is going to sleep; that is all. It Is not necessary that he should possess any peculiarity of temperament and voice, as has been supposed. In short, everything lies in the subject and not in the operator. Impress upon your subject the belief that what you say is about to happen, will happen, and you have paved the way to success. Give your subject to understand that you are perfectly competent to hypnotize him, and his imagination will do the rest. Assuming you are unable the get a person who has been under the influence before, I will ask you to secure a person (a stranger) who in your judgement would be easily influenced, — not one of those stubborn, over-confident know-it-all people, — but one who would be willing to obey your suggestions. The reason why some people are difficult to hypnotize is because they either consciously or unconsciously resist the operator's influence. They are not passive. Those between fifteen and twenty years of age are more easily controlled. Having secured your subject, place him in a chair in a comfortable position, preferably with his back to the light. Before you commence to operate it will be well to observe certain conditions. First, don't let anyone talk or laugh in the room while you are operating. Disturbing noises at the first tend to prevent hypnosis. They distract the attention, and thus interfere with the mental state for hypnosis. Later when you have, as well as your subject, learned to concentrate your thoughts, noises are less disturbing. The most absolute avoidance of any sign of mistrust by those is necessary, as the least word or gesture may thwart the attempt to hypnotize. Do not allow yourself to get excited, as there is nothing whatever to get excited about. Don't be afraid that you will have any trouble in awakening your subject as that is the easiest part of it, and there is absolutely no danger of being unable to bring the subject out of the hypnotic condition if you follow strictly what these lessons teach on the subject. Having observed the above precautions, you may now turn your attention to hypnotizing your subject. You have put him into a comfortable chair, and make sure that he is comfortable. Shift him about until he is resting easily, and say that he is resting. You do this for effect. Everything in this work depends upon the" effect you produce upon the subject's mind. You are not, while engaged in this work, a man of original thoughts; you are simply an actor, weighing tone and gesture, testing the effect of a glance, a sentence, a frown, a compression of the lips, a persuasive unbending; testing these things, weighing them, withdrawing them according to results, even as the regular physician tries and withdraws his material remedies according to results. Before beginning your work as the hypnotizer (no matter which method you use), your subject is to look at whatever you may request him to, and say to him that very soon he will become drowsy, then more and more drowsy, until he will be compelled to close his eyes and sleep. Be sure to tell him that he will notice nothing unusual about the drowsiness ; tell him that it will he just as pleasant as the approach to natural sleep that lie has ever experienced. Let him not expect anything unnatural to occur, for such will distract his attention and make him feel excited and less passive than he should be. Let him understand that it is for his good to be hypnotized if he is sick, or to help him cure a bad habit. Tell him that you will not make him appear ridiculous, and that you will only keep him asleep for a few minutes. Tell him to look earnestly at whatever you direct, and never under any circumstances to look away from it, no matter who comes into the room or around him he is going to gaze straight at the object and no other.

METHOD No. 1. — Take any bright object (I generally use my watch), between the thumb and fore and middle fingers of the right hand. Be sure that the light falls in the object in your hand. Hold it from eight to twelve inches from the eyes, at about ten inches above the head so as to produce the greatest possible strain upon the eyelids, and enable the subject to maintain a fixed steady stare at the object. The subject's eyes must be fixed steadily on the bright object, and his mind riveted upon the idea of the one object. When you notice the first change in your subject's face and eyes say such words as these: "Keep right on looking at it, directly you will be drowsy. You are sleepy. Your eyelids are heavy. You are asleep." Let your voice grow lower, lower, till just above a whisper. Pause a moment or two. Give him time. Never hurry. You will fail if you try to hurry too much at first. He will think it more natural if you give him a moment to get sleepy. Let him only listen. As soon as the eyelids really grow heavy, say: "Your eyes are almost closed now," making your words long drawn out and spoken in a tone which will not arouse him, but will, instead, indicate that you are yourself sleepy — and almost gone. Continue as follows: "Directly your eyes will have to close — you just cannot keep awake — see they are closing — now they are almost ready to close — now they will close and you will sleep. Close them-" Pause a moment, then say: "Sleep." Give the command to sleep in a quiet, yet firm and masterful way, in a low tone. You will see that the eyelids may quiver for a few seconds, sometimes for a minute, but very soon the subject will settle back in his chair, frequently with a sigh, and the eyes will become quiet, and his limbs show perfect relaxation. Let him remain so for some minutes, saying nothing to him at all. When you are ready to operate, it is well for you as a beginner, especially if you have a new subject, to constantly make suggestions. For instance, you say: "Nothing will wake you, nothing can hurt you. You can open your eyes, but you will stay asleep. Now I am about to raise your arm, but you won't wake up. Nothing will wake you." Rub the arm a few times and say: "Now you can't take it down — see, you can't. You are sound asleep, and you will do everything I tell you to do, but you will not wake up — you can't wake up till I tell you." The arm will remain in the position in which it is placed, and if you tell him that no person can take it down or bend it, you will find it true that no one can. I always begin operations in this way, placing both arms in an uplifted position, with both legs outstretched in the same manner. When you are ready to take them down rub them gently but firmly (rubbing from the body, and always raising the hands when reaching the extremities), and say: "Now you can take them down — see, you can — you will do all I tell you. You will have to do so. No one can wake you except myself." Speak to your subject just as though he were awake and in full possession of his senses. Although fast asleep to every one else, he is keenly awake to you. He went to sleep with his mind absorbed with the idea that you alone could control him, and this is the reason why no one else can make any impression on him. This connection between the subject and operator is called rapport, which is a state of sleep in which the attention of the subject is fixed exclusively upon the Hypnotist, so that the idea of him is constantly present in the subject's memory. It is possible, however, to put your subject en-rapport with any other person by simply suggesting to him to he is to obey the requests or demands of that person until further notice.

METHOD No. 2. — The subject reclines on a couch or easy chair, and you stand beside him. Hold the first two fingers of your right hand at a distance of about twelve inches from his eyes, at such an angle that his gaze shall be directed upwards in a strained manner. Direct him to look steadily at the tips of those fingers, and to make his mind as nearly blank as possible. After he has stared fixedly for about half a minute his expression will undergo a change — a far away look coming into his face. His pupils will contract and dilate several times, and his eyelids will twitch spasmodically. These signs indicate a commencement of the desired hypnotization. If the eyes do not close of themselves, shut them gently with your left hand, and say: "You are becoming sleepy; your eyes are very heavy; they are getting more and more heavy; my fingers seem quite indistinct to you (this when the pupils are observed to dilate or contract) ; a numbness is stealing over your limbs; you will be fast asleep in a few minutes; now sleep." This is a good method to use with children, and if they are hypnotized for any special reason hold their right hand with your left while talking to them.

METHOD No. 3. — Seat your subject if convenient in an ordinary chair (not an arm or rocking chair), with both feet flat upon the floor. Place his hands on his thighs with the palms down, the fingers pointed towards the knees. Then, standing three or four feet in front of him, request him to relax as much as possible, mentally and physically. Then say to him: "Look at one of my eyes," and draw his attention with the index finger of your right hand to the eye you wish him to look at. Lower your hand immediately to your side, and gaze directly and steadily into one of your subject's eyes until his pupil begins to dilate. This will require from five to ten seconds. Then repeat slowly the following: "Close your eyes gently — arch your eyebrows. Now you will find it hard to open your eyes. Try — try — try! All right, you may open them." Relax all tension in yourself when you say "All right." You must, of course, feel confident that you can hold his eyes closed for a few seconds. Your manner and tone should be such as to convince him that you can do so. As soon as you see that you have produced an impression at once release your subject for a moment. This will prevent his forming adverse auto-suggestions which might destroy the slight impressions already made. After a moment's rest, repeat the operation, saying again: "Look at one of my eyes. Close your eyes gently," and so on, just as before. Prom the moment you commence keep up a stream of oral suggestions, and repeat the above over and over again until you are quite sure your subject is under your influence.

How To Perform The Davenport Brothers' "Spirit Mysteries"

The "manifestations" of the Davenport Brothers are produced in either a cabinet or a darkened room, and in no instance while the operators are in full view of the audience. In a darkened room their "manifestations" mostly consist of the thrumming (without music) of guitars, ringing the bells, rattling of tambourines, etc., while at the same time the instruments are moved — as indicated by the sounds from them — with considerable rapidity about the room. The same sounds and movements also occur to a limited extent after the operators have been bound by a committee from the audience, the reintroduction of light disclosing them still in bonds as placed by the committee. They usually extricate themselves from the tying after the light is again extinguished, in less time than the committee occupied in binding them. During their entertainment they are also bound with ropes by what they assume to be a spirit power, without mortal assistance. To all appearance the tying done by "the spirits" is as methodical and secure as any that a mortal could do. Yet the very instant that darkness supervenes, after the knots have been examined by the committee, the musical instruments are sounded, and various "manifestations" made that could not possibly be accomplished without the use of hands; immediately on the cessation of which light is produced, and the "mediums" are ascertained to be bound as they were before the extinction of the light. Sometimes, while he is thus situated, one of the mediums will have his coat removed from his body in a few seconds' time. A performance of the Davenports, which many spiritualists have asserted to be an indubitable evidence of the exercise of spirit power, is as follows: One of them sits with his right side to the table on which the instruments are lying. The other takes a seat beside, and at the left of the one at the table. An investigator slt3 in front of the mediums, and puts a hand on the head of each; and, reaching up, each medium puts his hands, in separate places, but close together, on an arm of the investigator. The light is extinguished, and sounds are made on the instruments, the latter being moved, and perhaps brought in contact with the investigator's head. That gentleman is not conscious of any change in the position of the mediums. Their hands seem to him to remain constantly clasped to his arms, in which position they are found to be when the light is again produced. The mysterious cabinet in which the Davenports give their public exhibitions is about six feet high, six feet wide, and two and a half feet deep, the front consisting of three doors opening outward. In each end Is a seat with holes through which the ropes can be passed in securing the performers. In the upper part of the middle door ' is a lozenge-shaped aperture, curtained on the inside with black muslin or oil cloth. The bolts are on the inside of the door. As preliminary to the "manifestations," and in order that it may not be supposed that they are the operators, the mediums submit to being bound by a committee from the audience. The doors are then closed and bolted, it being necessary for the mortal manager to reach through the aperture to secure the middle door. A tremendous racket is soon made in the cabinet, the noise of the musical instruments being combined with a general whang banging and sometimes people in the audience think they can distinguish the sound of a cloven hoof kicking things around inside the structure which encloses the mediums. Usually, after the first performance, the doors of the cabinet are opened, and the committee requested to observe that the operators are still bound; but sometimes there is an interval just before the opening of the door, in which a rattling of the ropes is heard, and then the mediums walk forth, free. If they are observed by the committee before the ropes are removed from them, the doors are again closed till the untying is accomplished. Being again enclosed in the cabinet, the young men are bound by what they assert to be a spirit power, during the exercise of which they are passive. The 'spirit tying" is submitted for examination to the committee, by whom it is pronounced to be apparently so secure as to preclude the possibility of the mediums being able to use their hands. No sooner are the doors closed, however, than hands are seen at the aperture in the middle door. These hands are visible for but an instant at a time, and with a rapid vibratory movement while in view, so that it would not be possible for the observer to identify them as belonging to the mediums, however positively he might believe them to be theirs. Immediately on the disappearance of the hands from the aperture, the cabinet doors are opened, and the committee, after an examination, report the mediums to be still bound. The doors are again closed, and instantly "the spirits" strike up a lively tune on a violin, with a bell and tambourine accompaniment. That the audience may be still more profoundly impressed with the wonderful powers of the young men, they sometimes request that flour be placed in their hands, as a security, in addition to the "spirit tying," against their being able to use those members. Their request being complied with, a hand or two is shown at the aperture, some noises are made on the musical instruments, and then the mediums exhibit the flour still in their hands, with none spilled on their clothing' or the floor. Sometimes they permit one of the committee to sit in the cabinet with them, for a short time, while they are bound, but he. too, must be bound, with his right hand secured to one medium's shoulder, and his left hand to the other medium's knees. The lights in the hall are then turned down so that it is quite dark in the cabinet. The gentleman in contact with the mediums is banged over the head with an instrument of music, his hair is pulled, his nose tweaked, and altogether he is "pretty considerably mussed up." Being released from the not very pleasant position, and perhaps looking somewhat scared, he reports to the audience what has been done to him, with the additional statement that he did not detect any movement on the part of the mediums. "If not the manifestation of spirit power, what is it?" is a question which very naturally arises in the minds of those present. An answer is contained in the following explanations : In a darkened room, the investigators being seated by the walls, the mediums grasp the guitars by the neck, next the keys, and swing them around, and thrust them into different parts of the open space of the room, at the same time vibrating the strings of the instruments with the forefinger. The faster the finger passes over the strings, the more rapidly the instrument seems to move. Two hands can thus use as many guitars, and a tea-bell, clasped by the little linger of either hand, can be rung at the same time. Or one performer can sound a guitar and bell with one hand, and play an accordion or concertina with the other, an end of the last named instrument being held under the arm against the body. In the darkness the audience thinks the instruments go furthur than they really do: and the room being close, the sounds are echoed or reflected from the walls. When an investigator is sitting with the mediums at a table whereon musical instruments are lying, his hands resting on their heads, and their hands clasped to his arm above the elbow, the medium next the table removes one hand from the arm without being detected, simply because the presence of the other hand, which is nearer the shoulder, is so great as to cut off communication by means of the nerves of sensation from the arm below. It is thus impossible for the investigator to determine whether both hands of the medium are on his arm or not. He thinks they are, because the sensation in his arm remains the same. In the first place, the left hand of the medium is put heavily on the arm next the shoulder, and the right hand Quite lightly, close by the other next the elbow. Both hands are seen to be on the arm, and are presumed to be pressing with equal force. The light ia extinguished, and perhaps the medium takes the man's attention momentarily from his arm, by suggesting: that their feet be placed in contact; then it is that with a gradually increased pressure of his left hand the medium carefully removes his right hand, and while he preserves a rigidity of the muscles of his neck and back, so as not to move his head, he takes the guitar (which lies within reach) by the neck, and extending the body of the instrument as far as possible, moves it in a half-circle, vibrating the strings with his fore-finger. That the demonstration may be more striking, perhaps he hits the guitar against the head of the man with whom he is in contact. If he wishes to ring a bell at the same time, he can hold it with his little finger. He can sound, in turn, all the instruments lying on the table; then, carefully replacing his hand on the man's arm, he is ready to have a light produced. The other medium really holds on with both hands to the arm he has clasped, feeling sure that while he does so it cannot be interfering with the operations of "the spirits*' at the table. Should the medium put his right hand on top of the extended thumb of his left hand, with an appearance, to the investigator, of both hands being on his arm, the same results could be produced with loss risk of detection; for the presence of the thumb, where the right hand was seen to be, would lead the investigator to suppose, in the darkness, that the hand was still there. If in their dark seance, phosphorus having been put on the instruments, you should see a phosphoresent light very far above the stage, you may take it that the instrument which is heard is not where the light is seen, but that the phosphorus has been rubbed from the instruments, and some other put on a piece of card-board, which is attached to a folding rod and elevated in the darkness, to the desired position. To the Davenports, the extrication of themselves, after being bound by a committee, ia a brief and easy task. A simple "twist of the wrist" will convert a "square knot," usually considered the most secure, into two "half-hitches," through which the part of the rope they enclose can be easily slipped. With a little slack in the rope any ordinary knot can be made into a "slip-knot." It is hardly possible to bind a man without causing him pain, so that he cannot get a "slack" in the rope. The writer has been bound with ropes a great many times by people who were determined to make a "good job" of the trying, and not once has he failed to release himself, often in less time than was occupied in binding him. After the Davenports have been bound in their cabinets by a committee, and the doors of the structure are closed, they immediately set to work to loosen the knots next their wrists and extricate their hands, which they usually succeed in doing in a short space of time. In some instances one of them will have a hand at liberty as soon as the middle door is bolted, which he exhibits at the aperture, to be followed shortly by other hands; then both the mediums do their "level best" in making a noise with such instruments as they have at hand. Speedily getting their hands back in the ropes and drawing the knots close to their wrists, they make some additional noise with one or two instruments which they had so placed as to be still within their reach, and then give a signal for the opening of the doors. The knots are examined by the committee and reported to be "the same as they were;" the doors are again closed and the operatives release themselves entirely irom the ropes, untying every knot. Sometimes, after being tied by the committee, the mediums cannot readily extricate their hands and get them back as they were, in which case they do not have the doors open till all the knots are untied, it beinga better policy for them to wait till "the spirits" have tied them before making a show of hands or torturing the musical instruments. The important point with the Davenports. in tying themselves, is to have a knot next their wrists that looks solid, "fair and square," but which at the same time will admit of being slipped, so that they can g-et their hands out in a moment. There are several ways in which such a knot can bo formed, one of which is as follows : A square knot is loosely tied in the middle of a rope, then the ends of the rope are tucked through, in opposite directions, below the knot, and the latter is then drawn tight. There are then two loops, which are left just large enough for the passage of the hand through them. The ends of the rope are then put through the holes in the seat, and tied beneath, and also to the feet. Lastly the hands are put through the loops, and the knot drawn close to the wrist, coming between the latter. No novice in tying would suspect from the appearance of such a knot, and without taking particular pains in tracing the direction of the rope in forming it, that it could be slipped. As the hands of the mediums when thus tied are at their backs, close to the end of the cabinet, the committee cannot have a very good opporunity to observe the most important knot. The doors next the ends of the cabinet are first closed by the manager, and as the mediums are then concealed from view of the audience, they strain open the loops and are ready to use their hands as soon as the middle door is closed, which one of them instantly bolts on the inside. Then their hands are thrust under the curtain, which hangs over the aperture in the door, and exhibited to the audience; but as. before stated, the hands are exhibited but for an instant at a time, and with a vibratory motion of them; otherwise they might be recognized as belongingto the mediums. To make the hands look larg-e or small, they spread or press together the Angers. With that peculiar motion imparted to them, four hands at the aperture will appear to be half a dozen, or more, as two pennies, rubbed together between the balls of a person's thumbs, will present what appear to be the edges of three. A lady's flesh-colored kid glove, nicely stuffed with cotton, has sometimes been exhibited as the hand of a female spirit — a critical observation of it not being allowed. These mediums once exhibited what they doubtless supposed would look like the hand of a negro; but it was of uniform blackness, palm and all. At one of their entertainments, when, in addition to the exhibition of "spirit hands," a naked arm was protruded from the aperture an old lady, who, on account of the dimness of her vision, was permitted to stand cloie by the cabinet, saw, notwithstanding her defective sight, what made her exclaim, "Well, I declare ! They must practice vaccination in the other world, for I see marks of it on that spirit arm!" When the "spirit arm" was shown at another time, rope marks were seen on the wrist 1 It takes these mediums but a few seconds to get their hands back into loops, and draw the knots close to their wrists, ready to be examined by the committee. In making the music, one medium holds the violin in the manner usual with most players of that instrument, and with the little linger of the bow hand he clasps a bell, which rings in time with the music. The other medium h?ats the tambourine on his head or knees with one hand, while his other hand i's engaged in making a noise on something else. The performances of these young men are interesting on account of the ingenuity and expertness exercised by them, and would not be in the least objectionable were it not for their pretended "mediumship."

Electrical Psychology

The most easy, sure and direct mode to produce electro psychological communication is to take the individual by the hand, in the same manner as though you were going to shake hands. Press your thumb with moderate force upon the ulnar nerve, which spreads its branches to the. ring and little finger. The pressure should be nearly an inch above the knuckle, and in range of the ring finger. Lay the ball of the thumb flat and particularly crosswise so as to cover the minute branches of this nerve of motion and sensation. When you first take him by the hand, request him to place his eyes upon yours, and to keep them fixed, so that he may see every emotion of your mind expressed in the countenance. Continue this pressure for a half a minute or more. Then request him to close his eyes, and with your fingers gently brush downward several times over the eyelids, as though fastening them firmly together. Throughout the whole process feel within yourself a fixed determination to close them, so as to express that determination fully in your countenance and manner. Having done this, place year hand on the top of his head and press your thumb firmly on the organ of Individuality, bearing partially downward, and with the other thumb still pressing the ulnar nerve, tell him — you can not open your eyes! Remember, that your manner, your expression of countenance, your motions and your language must all be of the most positive character. If he succeed in opening his eyes, try it once or twice more, because impressions, whether physical or mental, continue to deepen by repetition. In case, however, that you cannot close his eyes, nor see any effect produced upon them, you should cease making any further efforts, because you have now fairly tested that his mind and body both stand in positive relation as it regards the doctrine of impressions. If you succeed in closing the subject's eyes by the above mode, you may then request him to put his hands on his head, or in any position you choose, and tell him, you can not stir them! In case you succeed, request him to be seated, and tell him, you can not rise; If you are successful in this, request him to put his hands in motion, and tell him, yon can not stop them! If you succeed, request him to walk the floor, and tell him, you can not cease walking ! And so you may continue to perform experiments involving muscular motion and paralysis of any kind that may occur to the mind, till you can completely control him, in arresting or moving all the voluntary parts of his system.

How To Make Persons At A Distance Think Of You

Let it be particularly remembered that "Faith" and concentration of thought are positively needful to accomplish aught in drawing others to you or" making them thirds of you. If you have not the capacity or understanding how to operate an electric telegraph battery, it is no proof that an expert and competent person should fail doing so; just so in this case; if faith, meditation, 01 concentration of thought fail you, then will you also fail to operate upon others. First, you must have a yearning for the person you wish to make think of you ; and secondly, you must learn to guess at what time of day or night, he may be unemployed, passive, so that he be in a proper state to receive the thought which you dispatch to him. If he should be occupied in any way, so that his nervous forces were needed to complete his task, h f s "Human Battery," or thought, would not be in a recipient or passive condition, therefore your experiment would fail at that moment. Or if he were under heavy narcotics, liquors, tobacco, or gluttonous influences, he could not be reached at such moments. Or, if he were asleep, and you operated to affect a wakeful mind or thought, you would fail again at the moment. To make a person at a distance think of you, whether you are acquainted with him or not, matters not; I again repeat, find out or guess at what moment he is likely to be passive; by this I mean easy and careless; then, with the most fervent prayer, or yearning of your entire heart, mind, soul, and strength, desire he may think of you; and if you wish him to think on any particular topic in relation to you, it is necessary for you to press your hands, when operating on him, on such mental faculties of your head as you wish him to exercise towards you. This demands a meagre knowledge of Phrenology. His "Feeling Nature" or "Propensities," you cannot reach through these operations, but when he once thinks of you, (if he does not know you he imagines such a being as you are), he can easily afterwards be controlled by you, and he will feel disposed to go in the direction where you are, if circumstances permit, and he is his own master, for, circumstances alter cases. I said you cannot reach his "Feeling-," but only hi3 "Thinking Nature," truly, but after ho thinks of you once, his "Feeling Nature" or propensities, may become aroused through his own organization. In conclusion on this topic, let me say, that if you wish the person simply to think of you, one operation may answer: but on the contrary, if you wish him to meet you, or go where you are, all you have to do is to persevere in a lawful and Christian manner to operate, and I assure you, in the course of all natural thing's, that is if no accident or very unfavorable circumstances occur, he will make his way towards you, and when he comes within sight, or reaching distance of you, it will be easy to manage him.

How To Charm Those Whom You Meet And Love

When you desire to make any one "Love" you with whom you meet, although not personally acquainted with him, you can very readily reach him and make his acquaintance, if you observe the foregoing instructions, in addition to the following directions: Suppose you see him coming towards you in an unoccupied mood, or he is recklessly, or passively walking past you, all that remains for you to do at that moment is to concentrate your thought and send it into him as before explained and. to your astonishment, if he was passive, he will look at you, and now is your time to send a thrill to his heart, by looking him carelessly, though determinedly, into his eyes, and praying with all your heart, mind, soul and strength, that he may read your thought, and receive your true Love, which God designs we should bear one another. This accomplished, and you need not and must not wait for a cold-hearted, fashionable, and popular Christian introduction; neither should you hastily run into his arms, but continue operating in this psychological manner; not losing any convenient opportunity to meet him at an appropriate place, when an unembarrassed exchange of words will open the door, to the one so magnetized. At this interview, unless prudence sanction it, do not shake hands, but let your manners and loving eyes speak with Christian charity and ease: wherever, or whenever you meet again, at the first opportunity grasp his hand, in an earnest, sincere, and affectionate manner, observing at the same time, the following important directions, viz.: — As you take his bare hand in yours, press your thumb gently, though firmly, between the bones of the thumb and forefinger of his hand, and at the very instant when you press thus on the blood vessels, (which you can before ascertain to pulsate,) look him earnestly and lovingly, though not pertly nor fiercely, into his eyes, and send dJl your heart's, mind's, and soul's strength into his organization, and he will be your friend, and if you find him not to be congenial, you have him in your power, and by carefully guarding against evil influences, you can reform him to suit your own purified. Christian, and loving taste.

Writing On The Arm

The conjuror's explanation was a great lesson in "spiritualism." I next asked him to elucidate the trick of writing on the arm. On the occasion of my visit to Mr. Forster, when the raps indicated the second pellet, he required the "spirit" present to write the initials on his bare arm. Mr. Forster placed his arm under the table for a moment, then rested it in front of a lamp burning on the table, and quickly rolled up the sleeve of his coat. The skin was without stain or mark. He passed his hand over it once or twice, and the initials of the names I had written on the second pellet seemed to grow on the arm in letters of crimson. "It's a trick I do every night. It goes with the audience like steam," said the conjuror. "Very simple. Well, suppose a name. What name would you like?" "Henry Clay," I replied. Down went the conjuror's arm under the table. In a few seconds he raised it and exposed the bare forearm without mark upon it. He doubled up his fist tightly so as to bring the muscles of the arm to the surface, and rubbed the skin smartly with his open hand. The letters "H. C." soon appeared upon it in well-defined writing of a deep red color. "There you have it, gentlemen; that's the blood-red writing. Very simple. All you have to do is to take a lucifer-match, and write on your arm with the wrong end of it. If you moisten the skin with a little salt water first, all the better. Then wet the palm of the other hand, rub your arm with it. Send up the muscles and the bloodred writing will come out. It will fade away in less than no time. If you look under the table, you will see that I have a little piece of pointed wood. I can move my arm under that and write the letters without using the other hand. But that's a trick which wants practice.

Made in the USA
Columbia, SC
13 March 2025